Praise

Performance

"If you have ever found yourself in a tough situation where doubt and insecurity were becoming your dominant thoughts, then this book is for you. A must-read for anyone searching for the answer to peak performance."

—JOHN NOBLES, CORPORATE DIRECTOR, LEADERSHIP & ORGANIZATION DEVELOPMENT, OWENS-ILLINOIS, INC.

"[Dr. Dallaire] provides simple yet powerful tools that take into account the nuances of individual personalities, helping the reader to build a self-tailored way to access one's best possible performance again and again. This book is a chance to get started on the road to getting the maximum out of one's gifts and talents."

—HARSHA A. SEN, MD, RETINAL SURGEON, SCIENTIST, AND AUTHOR

"The insight and understanding that I gained from reading this book has given me a new perspective on the importance of controlling my thinking. This book is simply brilliant . . . brilliantly written, brilliantly simple, brilliantly accessible and for sure, extremely helpful."

—YVES MORIZOT, FOUNDER & PRESIDENT, STAND 21

"For those of us in the performance business, [this book] is no longer preferential information! In his book, Dr. Dallaire shares not only his theory, but practical application that will leave you enlightened and empowered."

—RON FELLOWS, PROFESSIONAL RACING DRIVER AND CO-OWNER, CANADIAN TIRE MOTORSPORT PARK

"*Performance Thinking* is the definitive resource on how to take your personal performance to the next level. The proven process used by professional race car drivers, top athletes in many different sports, Hollywood actors, and corporate leaders is now available to you in one easy-to-read resource. The principles, concepts, and techniques discussed in this book will help you to better handle the stressful road blocks that life throws in your path every day and give you a practical set of tools to truly optimize your performance. This is a must-read."

—SIMON HAYES, FOUNDER AND PRESIDENT, PERFORMANCE PHYSIXX

"Dr. Dallaire brings proven principles that can increase anyone's performance by helping them learn how to more effectively focus on the task at hand. This book will help you be your best."

—J. TIMOTHY LIGHTFOOT, PH.D., OMAR SMITH ENDOWED PROFESSOR OF KINESIOLOGY, DIRECTOR, SYDNEY AND JL HUFFINES INSTITUTE FOR SPORTS MEDICINE AND HUMAN PERFORMANCE, TEXAS A&M UNIVERSITY

"This is a book that an engineer can appreciate and refer to because it incorporates standards with explanations . . . appealing to me since solutions are offered and explained in concise detail."

—TRACY KROHN, FOUNDER AND CEO, W&T OFFSHORE

"I have spent a lot of time studying 'methods' and seeking coaching to improve my performance. Your help has been the only one that actually 'took,' and did so in a big way. Thanks for putting all of this into a 'user manual for the human mind.' "

—CHARLIE PUTMAN, PROFESSIONAL RACING DRIVER AND CEO, PESCO, INC.

"Jacques' ACT model process provides not only a great framework for thinking about what factors impact performance, but incorporates concepts that I find I use everyday. I highly recommend it."

—ROB KAUFFMAN, CO-FOUNDER, PRINCIPAL, AND DIRECTOR, FORTRESS INVESTMENT GROUP, LLC; OWNER, RK COLLECTION; AND CO-OWNER, MICHAEL WALTRIP RACING

"I can honestly say that because of the in-depth, thought provoking concepts and mindset guidance I received . . . I was able to achieve more than I ever imagined. It's one thing to know what to do, but another to do it. This book enables me to have the tools at my fingertips, so there are no excuses."

—LYN ST. JAMES, PROFESSIONAL RACING DRIVER, MOTIVATIONAL SPEAKER, AND AUTHOR

"After only two days of applying [Jacques'] approach, my driving performance improved dramatically and I knocked 2 seconds off of my lap times. Jacques went from 'witch-doctor' to 'guru' in one weekend for me! Although your job and role may be different, you can apply the same approach to any task."

—RUSSELL SMITH, CO-OWNER, KINETIC SPEED SHOP AND KINETIC MOTORSPORTS

"No matter what business you are in, each and every day you must be prepared to perform at the top of your game. Performance Thinking, and the principles it teaches, gives you the tools and proper mindset to focus on the things that you can control and to not be distracted by the things you cannot control. From the highest levels of executive leadership to the team members making it happen in the trenches, Performance Thinking can transform the way an organization approaches their goals and objectives. In the end, the message is clear and simple, but it can and will help create extraordinary results."

—JOHN M. DOONAN, DIRECTOR OF MOTORSPORTS, MAZDA
NORTH AMERICAN OPERATIONS

"I have found that when I apply the principals of the ACT Model to the challenges that I undertake, the results are much more satisfying, regardless of the outcome. I know that I've conscientiously attempted to do the best I could do. I am excited about using the concepts presented in Performance Thinking as a training tool for young associates in my business. A conscientious application of the principals advocated in this book can be a real game changer. It has been for me!"

—CARL ROGERS, PRESIDENT, CARL ROGERS & ASSOCIATES –
PARK SOUTH GROUP

"This isn't a book, it's a map. Study it carefully and you will find your way back to your 'A' game, every time. As a business owner, driver, and father, I have found the concepts and techniques discussed in Performance Thinking to be relevant to every part of my life. The principles it touches on are universal."

—JONATHAN BENNETT, CEO, COMPOSITE RESOURCES, INC.;
OWNER/DRIVER, CORE AUTOSPORT

"As a professional cyclist at the World Tour level, physical preparation is obviously important. But the mental skills side of our sport is also a critical component of the success equation. The information that is presented in Dr. Jacques' new book 'Performance Thinking' digs deeply into the mind-set of the successful high performer and the ACT Model process I have been working with over the past months is proving to be the answer I have been seeking for some time. I know that this methodology will help me to achieve my highest performance goals!"

—TOM DANIELSON, PROFESSIONAL CYCLIST, TEAM GARMIN CERVELO

Performance THINKING

Mental Skills for the Competitive World ... and for Life!

JACQUES DALLAIRE, PH.D.

Dallaire Consulting LLC
Concord, NC

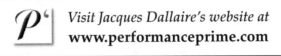

Visit Jacques Dallaire's website at
www.performanceprime.com

 www.facebook.com/performanceprime

 www.twitter.com/performprime

ISBN: 978-0-9851461-0-8

Published by Dallaire Consulting LLC, Concord, NC

Edited by Nancy Burke and Carol Rosenberg

Cover design & layout by The Book Couple
(Carol and Gary Rosenberg)

Produced in cooperation with The Book Couple
(www.thebookcouple.com)

Printed in the United States of America by United Graphics, Inc.

10   9   8   7   6   5   4   3   2   1

These endeavors are often a labor of love.
I love what I do and I sometimes joke with people
that I have the best job in the world. The strange and
yet wonderful thing is that I really believe it! But the process
is never simple or easy. As with virtually everyone, there have
been a number of "B" factors that have gotten in the way
of our progress over the years, but I and my tribe have
managed to get through them by sticking together
and staying focused on what mattered.

To my wonderful children, Dom, Danielle, Luc, and Jessie,
thank you for doing your part and for always being supportive.
To my wife and partner, Fern, a special thank-you for being
there and hanging in from the very first step of this journey
together. I love you all. This book is dedicated to you.

Contents

PART THREE

The *A.C.T. Model©* Process: Reprogramming Your Mind to Optimize Your Personal Performance

Foreword

When I first heard about Performance Prime in 2008, I had already made the personal decision to spend more time and effort to become a competitive race car driver. My friends and co-drivers Joe Foster and Charles Espenlaub had both participated in the Performance Prime program and were keen to share information and techniques they learned while working with Dr. Jacques Dallaire. I got to know Jacques informally over the next year and although my crazy schedule prevented me from actually participating in the program until 2009, I understood early on that this practical information would have a direct, positive impact on my racing performance. I quickly realized that his unique approach would also be highly relevant to my work life as an actor and to my life in general. I knew that the knowledge and tools that I would acquire would help me to achieve my personal performance goals across the board.

Through testing, Jacques evaluated my mental skills and profiled my strengths and weaknesses. He also helped me establish a personal performance model—an A.C.T. Model—that I could use to actively control my thinking when it came time for me to perform. I realized going through this process that I never *really* understood how I sabotaged myself. Apparently everyone does it, and I am no exception. Over time, I learned how to shift my thinking in these moments of self-sabotage and as a result, how to control my dominant thought so that I can deliver the best performance that I am capable of, regardless of the challenges that the situation presents. In addition, I learned to recognize and effectively reinforce the correct performance-relevant thinking I have used in the past and integrate it into my day-to-day life.

As a husband, parent, actor, producer, and race car driver, I have applied the A.C.T. Model process to the many different facets of my life. While there are some differences in the way that I apply this thinking process for these different roles, there is a common underlying theme that makes me "tick" when I am in the "Zone." It may seem like an overwhelming challenge to change self-limiting habits but it is not as difficult to apply as you may think. The process is very "doable"; it just requires a different way of thinking, and I am proof that it can be done!

To this day, I rely on my A.C.T. Model to deal with the challenges of a busy and demanding schedule. It continues to have a meaningful effect on my performance as it helps me to more effectively "get out of my own way"—I now clearly understand how to get the most out of myself whenever I perform. In fact, I got so much out of the program personally that I asked Jacques to come to California and share with members of my family and a few close friends, some aspects of his proven process that I find so powerful.

With so many things going on in our busy lives, it is easy to become distracted and allow the wrong kind of thinking to affect our performance in a negative way. Life's trials and tribulations can shake our confidence and this self-doubt can have a corrosive effect on our health and also on our ability to perform. The A.C.T. Model has truly helped me to develop the kind of confidence and task-focus that I aspire to, regardless of the job I am doing. It has become clear to me that worrying about the things I can't control while I am engaged in a performance is directly counterproductive when trying to deliver my best work.

The material in this book will help you to clearly understand *how* you mentally sabotage yourself. As you work through the final section of the book where you develop your own A.C.T. Model, you will learn how to neutralize this natural human tendency. This methodology is not a magic solution, however. It requires discipline to control your thinking, but the rewards are great if you do. I encourage you to actively focus as you read this material. The interactive exercises this book offers will allow you to gain insight into your underlying performance mind-set. It is my hope that you will get as much out of this book as I have, and I believe that the effort and time you invest to develop these mental skills will be well worth it. It could also be life-changing.

—Patrick G. Dempsey

Acknowledgments

First, I would like to recognize the important role that my late friend and business partner, Dr. Dan Q. Marisi, played in helping to create the basic programs and processes that I have adapted and continued to utilize since his passing in 1999. We started this journey together in 1983 under a university-based program that we called "The Motor Sport Research Group at McGill University," and created an approach and specific tools that truly were unique in the world of performance training at the time. Even today, the approach we utilize is significantly different from anything that is being done in the high-performance training marketplace anywhere in the world. It is an approach that has proven to be highly effective over decades and while I continue to refine the delivery model for the process we have been using, I feel no need to reinvent the wheel. Since the process works so well, we simply continue to apply it.

Second, I want to thank the many high-performance clients and colleagues with whom I have worked over the years. They have openly shared their views, experiences, and insights about the challenges and unique characteristics that exist in the high-performance world and have taught me as much as, if not more than, I hope that I have been able to teach them.

I would also like to recognize the invaluable assistance of The Book Couple, Carol and Gary Rosenberg, who have provided editorial, design, and production support as the book made its way through the maze that is the self-publishing process. Nancy Burke completed the final editing of the manuscript and the folks at United Graphics produced the printed version of the book and put it into my hands. Thank you for your help and your professional work.

And finally, I want to extend a special thank you to my exceptional team of pre-readers! These very accomplished individuals took time out of their busy schedules to help me to make this book the best that it can be. Each one of them enthusiastically agreed to read the manuscript and give me candid feedback regarding the story that I wanted to tell and the voice that I chose to tell it. They agreed to help me in this endeavor because:

• They know that the material is relevant to everyone,

• They are confident the process works (because they or someone close to them has used it), and

• They recognize that in these challenging times, each of us can use this information to reduce the amount of negative stress that we feel, and to improve our personal performance.

I appreciate your help and support more than you know . . .

Jonathan Bennett, Founder & CEO, *Composite Resources, Inc.;* Owner/Driver, *CORE Autosport*

Narvel Blackstock, President, *Starstruck Management Group*

T. Mark Buford, Senior Vice President & Corporate Controller, *Community Health Systems, Inc.*

Helio Castroneves, Professional Racing Driver; Three-time Indy 500 Champion; 2007 *Dancing With the Stars* Champion

André Dallaire, Maintenance Section Leader, *Exxon-Mobil Chemical Corporation*

Tom Danielson, Professional Cyclist, *Team Garmin Cervelo*

Patrick Dempsey, Multi Award-Winning Television & Motion Picture Actor; Co-Owner/Driver, *Dempsey Racing*

John Doonan, Director of Motorsports, *MAZDA North American Operations*

Charles Espenlaub, Professional Racing Driver; CEO, *Safecraft Racing*

Richard Fant, CEO, *New Process Steel, Inc.*

Ron Fellows, Professional Racing Driver; Co-Owner, *Canadian Tire Motorsport Park*

Joe Foster, Professional Racing Driver; Co-Owner/Driver, *Dempsey Racing*

Alex Glasscock, Founder & CEO, *The Ranch at Live Oak Malibu*

Patrick Gonsalves, Senior Sales Professional, *Q107—Corus Entertainment*

John Gorsline, Founder & CEO, *The Gorsline Company*

Bill Griswold, Chairman—Charlotte, NC, *Vistage International, Inc.*

Steve Hallam, Managing Director, *Walkinshaw Racing*

Simon Hayes, President, *Performance Physixx*

Jim Jordan, Alternative Marketing Manager, *MAZDA North American Operations*

Rob Kauffman, Cofounder, Principal, and Director, *Fortress Investment Group;* Co-Owner, *Michael Waltrip Racing*

Richard Klein, Vice President, Manufacturing & Engineering— *GSM, Stanley Black & Decker, Inc.*

Tracy Krohn, Founder, Chairman, & CEO, *W&T Offshore*

Jim Leo, Founder & President, *PitFit Training, Inc.*

Patrick Long, Professional Racing Driver

J. Timothy Lightfoot, Ph.D., Omar Smith Endowed Professor of Kinesiology; Director, *Sydney and JL Huffines Institute for Sports Medicine and Human Performance, Texas A&M University*

Reba McEntire, Multi Award-Winning Musical Entertainer, Actress, and Author; Country Music *Hall of Fame* Inductee

Jamie McMurray, Professional Racing Driver

Yves Morizot, Founder & President, *Stand 21*

John Nobles, Corporate Director, Leadership & Organization Development, *Owens-Illinois, Inc.*

Andy Pilgrim, Professional Racing Driver; CEO, *Electronic Computer Services, Inc.*

Charlie Putman, Professional Racing Driver; CEO, *PESCO, Inc.*

Carl Rogers, President, *Carl Rogers & Associates—Park South Group*

Harsha A. Sen, M.D., Retinal Surgeon, Scientist, and Author

Bruce Silver, Founder & CEO, *Racing Electronics, Inc.*

Marcus Smith, Chief Operating Officer & President, *Speedway Motorsports Inc.;* General Manager, *Charlotte Motor Speedway*

Russell Smith, Co-Owner, *Kinetic Speed Shop; Kinetic Motorsports*

Lyn St. James, Professional Racing Driver, Motivational Speaker, & Author

Craig Stanton, Professional Racing Driver

Richard L. Sutherland, President and CEO, *ClickAway Corp.*

Terry Trammel, M.D., Orthopedic Surgeon and Partner, *Orthopaedics Indianapolis, Inc.;* Founding Member, *International Council of Motorsport Sciences;* Fellow, *FIA Institute for Motorsport Safety*

Peter von Moltke, CEO, *UBM Aviation, Inc.*

Cal Wells III, Former CEO, *Michael Waltrip Racing*

Introduction

I have been in the fortunate position over the past forty years to interact with and influence literally thousands of high-performance individuals involved in a broad variety of sports and high-risk/high-demand occupations. Many of these people have been leaders in the business and occupational world, and champions in their respective competitive sports. I have learned much from these top professionals regarding the *real* world of high performance and the unique demands and challenges that exist in that world. My professional life has been dedicated to sharing with them insights and training strategies that they could then use to help them achieve and even exceed their performance goals.

This book distills the practical experience that I have gained over the years and integrates it with the knowledge that I acquired through my formal education and training in exercise physiology, together with things that I learned from my late business partner and friend, Dr. Dan Marisi. Dan had a Ph.D. in Sport and Educational Psychology and was himself a high-performance athlete at one time in his life. Together, we created many of the early processes and the approach that I have continued to develop since his passing in 1999.

I, with the invaluable help of my group of "pre-readers" (every one of them an accomplished high performer in their own right), have made every effort to make this book both readable and practical. I did not want to create a reference book loaded with scientific jargon or technical explanations as to why things are the way they are. When I do reference research, it is only to explain a concept that I believe is worth knowing in greater detail, and in those instances I have attempted to do so in an understandable manner.

 The basic intent of this book seeks to answer the fundamental and universal questions: *How do I mentally sabotage my own performance?* and *How can I learn not to?*

Note that I have highlighted these questions by using a stylized icon (*P'*). I will utilize this icon throughout the book to highlight **key points** or **concepts** that I want to reinforce as being particularly important from my perspective. I intend to use it sparingly so you will recognize that the point associated with the icon is worthy of special focus as you work your way through the material.

My goal in writing this book is to help you, the reader, become more effective at delivering your "A" game, regardless of the arena in which you are called upon to perform. In my experience, you will have a better chance of figuring out the answers to these two important questions if you understand the problem more clearly. I set out in the first part of the book to explain how the process of mental self-sabotage begins, how it evolves, and exactly how it impacts your ability to perform. We cover a lot of background information in the first section, but I believe that this broader and deeper discussion will bring greater clarity to the issues that truly impact your performance. I also believe that it will allow you to cement the concepts in your mind more firmly so that you will be better able to remember and integrate them into your thinking going forward.

You will note that I have included a small printed card tucked into the first few pages of this book. This card lists the *Rules of the Mental Road©* that we will discuss in the second part of the book. I encourage you to use it as a handy reference as you work your way through the material. It will help you to remember the Rules and better understand how they fit together as a framework for **Performance** *Thinking*. You will also be able to keep the card with you as a handy reminder after you have finished reading the book.

I want to be clear from the outset however, so that there is no confusion. This book is *not* about the power of positive thinking. While positive thinking is most definitely better than negative thinking in terms of optimizing your performance, in the high-performance world, positive thinking is just not good enough by itself. More is needed. Each of us knows people who are positive indeed but who cannot perform very well when the chips are down and it is "go" time. I have encountered many such individuals throughout my career as a performance specialist who are very positive people, who are happy, and who see life's glass as being half-full, but they do not perform particularly well on a consistent basis. Delivering excellence is not about spouting thoughtless platitudes with *no process* in place to help cement and sustain the mind-set necessary to perform at our best.

What this book *is* about, is understanding how our mind works as it relates to basic mental skills and how these thought processes affect our ability to perform. It is also about the power and methodology of our *dominant thought* and how positive and productive thinking allows us to gain control over our mind in a way that optimizes our personal performance, as opposed to sabotaging it.

I am confident that the information I will share with you throughout this book can help you to improve your personal performance, regardless of the specific occupation in which you work or the sport that you play. I will discuss the basic mental skills that underlie your ability to perform as a human being as well as how to begin to better control your dominant thought so that your mind-set is more consistently positive and productive, rather than negative and destructive. As most of us probably realize, in many cases *we* are our own worst enemy and what we really need to do is to learn how to get out of our own way! If we can control our thoughts, we can learn how to perform "in the moment" and in so doing express the full extent of our talents, unencumbered by the destructive mind-set that so often grips us as we face our most significant and challenging obstacles.

My primary goal in writing this book is to provide food for thought. I intend to share with you a number of useful concepts and discuss some basic mental rules that, if abided by, can change your ability to perform in profound ways. They may even change your life. They are simple enough in concept but not automatic when it comes time to implement them in real life. This is because they require discipline and clarity of understanding to be able to use them to systematically shape and control your thinking in the most challenging situations.

This book is intended to focus on the mental skills that influence behavior and personal performance at the competitive end of the spectrum. To this end, I will utilize examples drawn from all over the map: the world of business, high-risk/high-demand occupations, and high-performance sport to discuss the various principles of mental training that are relevant to each example. This approach will shed light on the universality of these principles. I am confident that you will quickly become aware that this information applies as much to your everyday life as it does to your performance in the work environment, regardless of the role that you play within that environment.

In addition, you will also recognize that it applies equally to your children and to other family members, whether they are involved in competitive sport or in the performance arts. Beyond the high-performance world, these concepts and principles underpin critical life skills that cut across all boundaries. We can indeed identify the characteristics within high-performance people that help to make them successful and model these thought processes and behaviors in our lives as well, to influence us in a positive way. Indeed, over the years, this universal applicability has resonated with all of the clients that I have worked with.

In the first section of the book (Part One) we will consider several important concepts that serve as the basis for the discussion that follows. In Chapter 1, I dive right into the subject matter to consider—with some real-world examples—what the "Performance Equation" reveals about how the way that we think directly influences our ability to perform. This chapter forms a necessary foundation that we will build upon as we flesh out additional important concepts in subsequent chapters in this section. The first four chapters frame the underlying concepts that help explain why the *Rules of the Mental Road©* are what they are.

I begin our discussion in Chapter 2 by considering how the human mind processes information at its most basic level. My goal here is not to delve into a complicated discussion of neurophysiology or neuropsychology, but rather to try to make sense out of how the mind manages information at its most basic level and how central processing function affects performance. Within this chapter, we will also examine basic principles regarding how the *conscious* and *unconscious* mind work and how these thought processes directly and indirectly affect our ability to perform.

In Chapter 3, we will discuss how *imagery* serves as the basis for virtually all of the mental skills that shape our emotions and behaviors. As you will soon recognize, *imagery* is indeed the *language of the mind* and as such, it serves as a powerful force to help or hinder our ability to perform.

In Chapter 4, we will consider the critical skill of *concentration* from a variety of perspectives. I believe firmly that the holy grail of the performance equation—the most important single feature that differentiates moments of personal brilliance from the many other instances of less-than-optimal performance—is our ability to effectively focus "in the moment" on the task at hand. This task-focus exists to the exclusion of everything else that is not relevant to our performance in that moment. This chapter will help you to understand what concentration is, and how controlling your focus of attention is the key to performing at the highest levels.

In Part Two of the book, beginning with Chapter 5, we will discuss the seven key *Rules of the Mental Road©*. These rules serve as a practical framework for **Performance *Thinking***. Using this framework, we will begin to examine how our mind works in straightforward, practical terms, and how these thought processes directly affect our performance.

The final section of the book (Part Three) answers the important question: "So now that I understand how I sabotage myself, how do I change?" The *A.C.T. Model©* process that I walk you through will answer that question.

In the final chapters of the book, I will introduce you to the process that I helped develop and have successfully delivered with high-performance athletes and numerous other professionals over many years. This process blends the best elements from a number of recognized psychological and mental training approaches and offers a practical framework to help you to deliberately shape and control your dominant thought. With such control, your mind-set will consistently be both positive and task-focused, whether things are going well or not. The A.C.T. Model© process has proven to be highly effective in helping individuals to achieve their best performances because it is based on a set of personal standards of excellence that are defined by each individual. Be forewarned, however! While the process integrates the key *Rules of the Mental Road©* and offers a solution that is simple and highly effective, it does require work to live it.

The A.C.T. Model© represents a beginning. Of all the things of value that I believe this book offers, this is the most important from my perspective. If you incorporate the A.C.T. Model© process into your life, you will be well on your way to gaining that elusive, yet critical mental skill that all high-performance people constantly seek—that of mental toughness. If you model the process consistently and attempt to integrate it into your performance on a day-to-day basis, you will develop a mental skills tool kit that will serve you well both in the competitive world and in life in general.

As we prepare to take this journey together, consider for a

moment what it would mean to you if you were able to consistently control your mind in such a way as to *allow yourself* to deliver your very best performance in the face of every major challenge you tackle in your life (for example, the "big" meeting; the "big" event; the "big" game; the "big" . . .). Just imagine the possibilities.

AN OVERVIEW

The Seven Key *Rules of the Mental Road*©

RULE #1   If you want to climb out of a hole, the very first thing you must do is *stop digging*!

If you want to think positively, first you must stop thinking negatively. Sometimes we dig ourselves into a mental hole by thinking negative thoughts. These negative thoughts gain strength and power the more we process them and before we know it, we are staring at the bottom of a hole and digging furiously. We end up so far down that hole of negative thinking that we cannot seem to find our way out. If you want to shift your mind-set to positive and productive thinking, you first must *choose* to process only positive and productive thoughts. If you do not consciously, actively, and deliberately stop digging, you will not be able to shift your dominant thought to the kind of positive and productive thinking you need to turn yourself around and climb out of the hole.

RULE #2   The mind can only actively process *one* thought *at a time.*

No matter how hard you try to think about two thoughts *at the same time,* you cannot do it! We cannot actively process two thoughts at the same time, but we can shift back and forth from one thought to another, in a multitasking mode. What is the implication of this rule from a performance point of view? It is simple. If you are focused on this (whatever "this" is), you cannot be focused on that (whatever "that" is) *at the same time.*

RULE #3 You can't *not* think about *whatever is on your mind.*

What generally happens when you tell yourself not to get nervous, not to get angry, and not to mess up? Quite often, exactly what you wanted *not* to do is exactly what you do, exactly the way you pictured it in your mind's eye! That is because the mind *cannot act positively* in response to a negative thought. Think about this carefully: what is the consequence of flooding your mind with negative thoughts? The answer: you become negative and your focus of attention shifts to the wrong thing at the wrong time. Since you can't *not* think about whatever is on your mind, it is essential that you control your dominant thought when you perform.

RULE #4 Your *dominant thought* determines your emotions, the behaviors that flow from those emotions, and ultimately, your ability to perform.

Your dominant thought is translated into action through the work of your unconscious mind. This is why imagery is such a powerful tool in shaping your emotions, your behaviors, and ultimately, your ability to perform. Often, however, we implant dominant thoughts in our mind that are negative and counterproductive to our best performance. Rule #3 tells us that we *can't not think* about whatever thought is dominant within our mind. You must ensure that the *dominant thought* you choose to focus on is one that will contribute to your ability to perform, rather than take away from it.

RULE #5 You *are in control* of your dominant thought.

You cannot control the events that occur around you (like winning or what other competitors might do), but you are always 100 percent in control of *how you respond* to the situation in front of you. You can choose to spin out of control and focus on the negative, or you can "reframe" the event and look for the opportunity in it. You might be surprised to find that in most cases, there is opportunity if you look for it. Even in the most difficult circumstances, the situation always presents you with an opportunity to measure yourself against difficult challenges, to rise to the occasion, to exhibit a champion's mind-set, and to learn from the experience.

RULE #6   Your *perception* or *perspective* regarding the challenges that you face will determine your emotional response. Choose your perception carefully!

It is not the difficult events in your life and your sport or occupation that cause you stress. It is your interpretation (your perception or perspective) regarding those events that can lead to a stress response that is negative and counterproductive to your performance or positive, to energize and motivate you to put in the effort needed to become a champion. Perception ultimately takes place in the brain, not in the eyes. Therefore, what we see is only our mind's interpretation of what is actually there. Change your perspective on the challenges that you face on a daily basis and you will change your stress response. In those situations where you are mentally and emotionally struggling with the challenges in your life, the feedback or input of a trusted mentor or professional can be very helpful in putting a different perspective on the situation. Do not neglect to consider these options if appropriate.

The glass of water that one person sees as being half-empty is the same glass that another person sees as being half-full. It is a matter of perspective—one that is influenced by your belief as to whether you are filling it or drinking from it. An active and purposeful *shift in your thinking* can have a positive effect on your performance and your health.

RULE #7   If you do what you have always done, you will get what you have always gotten. If you want something different, you must approach the challenges that you face with a different mind-set!

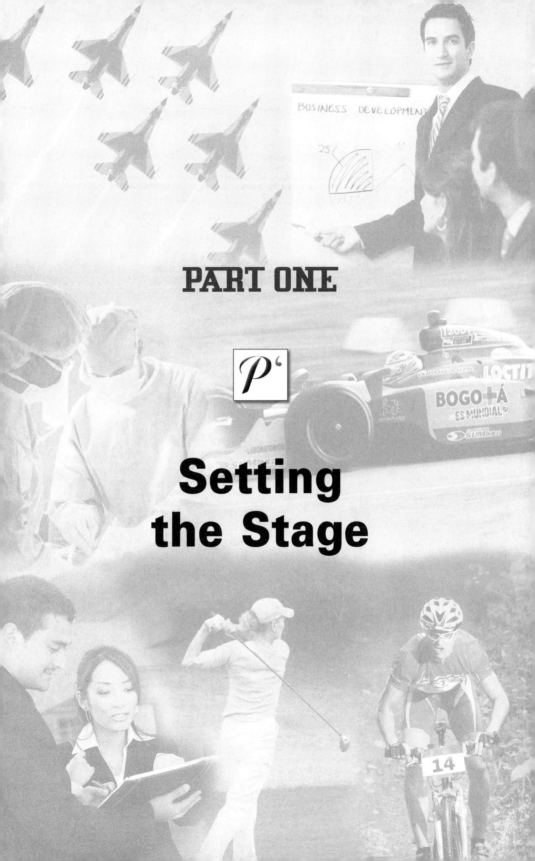

PART ONE

Setting the Stage

CHAPTER 1

Performance: "A" x "B" = Results

Success has a simple formula;
do your best and people may like it.

—SAM EWING, ATHLETE & BUSINESSMAN

Success is blocked by concentrating on it and planning for it . . .
Success is shy—it won't come out while you're watching.

—TENNESSEE WILLIAMS, AUTHOR & DRAMATIST

Don't aim for success if you want it; just do what you love
and believe in it and it will come naturally.

—DAVID FROST, JOURNALIST

Sometimes your personal performance can only be described as spectacular—moments of brilliance where everything just goes right! Your focus is on target and your mind is sharp, easily processing the information that allows you to bring your "A" game to the event, regardless of what that event might be. You possess a relaxed confidence that facilitates dealing with any challenge or problem that might arise. You can almost tell what is going to happen even before it happens. Your performance seems effortless, even though your energy level is high. It is one of those all-too-rare "Yes!" moments. You are in your mental "zone" of best performance . . .

But then again, sometimes you're not . . .

Why is it that in some situations, your performance truly is the best you are capable of doing while in others, you struggle and just cannot seem to get into the mental groove where you do your best work? We have all experienced these situations where our ability to perform varies, sometimes even dramatically. Even though we cannot always put our finger on why it happens, we know that it is *not* because we forget, from one time to the next, what it takes to excel.

In these pages, we are going to completely peel back the layers of the onion, revealing the answers to this conundrum. In so doing, you will soon come to recognize that the fundamental reason that we experience these major swings in personal performance (you will note here that I did not say "results") lies in our inconsistent application of key basic mental skills that underlie our ability to perform as human beings. This occurs whether the performance is in the boardroom, on the sales floor, on the golf course, or wherever.

When my clients participate in my comprehensive *Individual Performance Program,* I ask every one of these high performers what they hope to gain from the experience. Stated another way: what is it that they would like to change about themselves that they know holds them back from bringing their very best performance to their event? Now remember, many of the individuals I have worked with over the years are top performers in their respective professions, including company executives and entertainers, as well as world-class athletes in many sports. Take a moment to reflect on the following question with respect to yourself:

If you could change one *thing about yourself that you know would have a positive and maybe even a profound effect on your ability to perform in challenging situations, what would* you *want to change? Take a few moments to think about this before you read on . . .*

Would it surprise you to find out that within thirty seconds, more than 90 percent of my clients reply to this question with at least one of the same two answers, and often with both! It does not matter what profession or sport they are involved in, what culture they are from, what language they speak, whether they are male or female, or how old they are, virtually every one of these individuals seems to be looking for the same things. The two main requests I have heard from these highly successful performers over the years have been:

 "Show me how to maintain my *confidence* when things are not going well," and "Show me how to *focus* more effectively, and when I lose focus, how to get it back quickly."

Isn't it interesting? It does not matter what business they are in, the same two issues appear to be centrally important to their ability to perform. In fact, these two requests provide us with a powerful clue to one of the fundamental secrets behind why high-performance people become successful. Through my program, these clients are seeking to learn how they can express their talents fully within their performances without the self-sabotaging mind-set that often shackles competitive people. We will tackle the second of these issues (the question of *focus*) in Chapter 4 as a stand-alone element, since it is arguably the holy grail of the performance equation.

Let us address the other key issue now: "Show me how to maintain my confidence when things are not going well." How is it that many of the most successful business professionals and athletes out there today seem to wrestle with this issue of confidence? Are these not the most confident and focused individuals you can think of? And yet, when we drill down to the core of it, this is what they are looking for. Should it really surprise us then that we too often wrestle with this very same issue? Let me share with you a basic truth that I have consistently observed over the years with thousands of individuals in the high-performance domain:

It is relatively easy to be confident and have a positive mind-set when things are going well . . .

Wow, isn't that a surprise! Not really. We have all been there—when things are going well, it is relatively easy to maintain confidence and have a positive mind-set. The true champion, however, is someone who is able to preserve a strong sense of self-confidence even when the results they seek are not being realized. In so doing, they retain their ability to deliver their best performance, regardless of the magnitude of the challenges that they face and the potential consequences of failure. High-level competitors understand this and it explains why this is a critical part of their **Performance *Thinking*** approach.

But what is it that causes us to sometimes lose confidence, resulting in a state of mind that negatively affects our personal performance in often dramatic ways? To understand how this comes about, we first need to consider what for many individuals serves as the yardstick by which they define success, and around which they build their personal confidence.

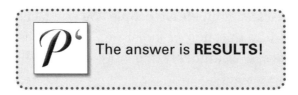

The answer is **RESULTS!**

So often, we allow our confidence to be dictated by the results that we achieve . . . or fail to achieve. When results are good, it is relatively easy to maintain a high level of self-confidence. On the flip side, when results are poor, confidence often takes a beating and our personal performance suffers. This argument seems sound in conceptual terms, but let us consider the example of a generic sales associate to further explore this issue of self-confidence and its ultimate effect on performance.

What do you think happens to a salesperson's self-confidence when, for the tenth call in a row, they fail to register a single sale?

In situations like this, the poor result can sometimes destroy the individual's confidence. They begin to doubt themselves as they move on to the next sales call and wonder whether they are the cause of their perceived failure. They begin to worry about whether they will ever be able to climb out of this performance hole they seem to be in, and their concern builds. They desperately want to generate good results, but they gradually develop a sense of pessimism regarding their ability to "close" the deal; and this negative mind-set infects their thoughts and their subsequent behaviors and actions. They move on to their next sales call with a higher degree of anxiety and even with an expectation of failure. This becomes a self-fulfilling prophecy that has a greater chance of being realized because of their dominant negative mind-set. Add to this growing problem the fact that their boss may be constantly applying pressure to "make it happen."

 This combination can subsequently cause their *focus* to shift away from what they should be focused on to the source of their worry.

In this example, however, the results that the salesperson obtained may have had little or nothing to do with the personal performance they are self-evaluating so critically. For a number of those sales calls, marketplace forces may have had a direct impact on the ability of their targeted prospects to take action and place an order, even though the proposition was interesting and well presented. On other occasions, potential clients may have been looking for a highly specialized product that was not part of the company's current or planned inventory, and the correct fit was simply not there. Another potential explanation might be that the terms these potential clients were insisting on were totally unrealistic given the quality of the product being offered, the cost of goods, and a reasonable profit margin. Regardless, the bottom line remains: the salesperson in this example failed to register even a single sale!

When *you* lose your confidence, is it tough to climb out of that mental hole you dig yourself into? You bet it is! Each of us has been there before and we know just how difficult it is to turn that kind of negative thinking around. One of the greatest challenges we face in these types of situations is to avoid defining our confidence primarily on the basis of the results that we achieve. That is because the fundamental truth of the matter is that more often than not,

We *cannot* directly determine or control results!

No matter how well you might perform individually, in most instances there are factors outside of your control that have a direct effect on the outcome of your performance. In the example described above, in each situation where the salesperson failed to make a sale, factors leading to this result may very well have been outside of his direct control. His personal performance in these situations could even have been superlative, but other factors may have negatively affected the outcome. When you allow results to define the level of confidence that you feel in these challenging moments, the lack of results can lead to a performance slump that can have a serious effect on your livelihood and your career. Failure has a way of turning us into pessimists and we often develop a mind-set over time that expects the worst to occur. This becomes a self-fulfilling prophecy that leads us to expect failure, just the way that we imagined it.

Now substitute the above scenario with some other situation where *you* might be called upon to perform in your work or sport environment and where the results at the end of the day are not what you had hoped that they would be. But how do we put this situation into proper perspective? Consider the **Performance Equation** that follows:

$$\text{"A" x "B" = Results}$$

In this simple equation, **Results** are the product of two variables: **"A"** and **"B"**. Let us substitute the phrase "My Performance" for the "A" variable in our equation and the phrase "All the Factors Outside of My Control" for the "B" variable. Keep in mind that this is not intended as a mathematical equation . . . it is a conceptual one. It now reads:

$$\text{My Performance } x \text{ All the Factors Outside of My Control}$$
$$= \text{ Results}$$

Our personal performance—which is defined by our current level of skill and experience, our talent, the knowledge we possess at the moment of that performance, our desire and commitment to work diligently, and so on—is only *one* of the variables that influences the results that we are capable of achieving as we tackle the many challenges of our life. Factors that are truly outside of our control (such as: what competitors might do; what other people choose to think; marketplace forces; equipment failure; legislative or regulatory changes; luck, and so forth) can and most often do have a direct influence on results. It is just part of life—sometimes we are the windshield and sometimes we are the bug! While we might understand the fundamental truth of this relationship intellectually, we consistently seem to forget it when we (and sometimes others) evaluate our personal performances.

We are taught in school and throughout most of our lifetime that hard work and perseverance will lead us to success. However, the harsh reality is that this is not always the case, and to some degree, we have been sold a false proposition in the name of motivation. Sometimes, in spite of our best efforts, things do not always work out. The older we get, the more we recognize the truth of this statement. We come to realize that those pesky "B" factors in the Performance Equation do sometimes prevent us from achieving the goals we had originally set for ourselves. Some people call this acquired clarity of thought "wisdom." There is however, one thing of which you can be certain—given the basic truth of this simple equation:

 If you give *less than your best performance* as you take on a particular challenge, the results you achieve in that situation will be less *than they could have been.*

If the "A" in our equation is actually an "A–", the result will likely be less than optimal. On the other hand, if you deliver your best performance (a full-on "A" game performance), the result you achieve will be as great as it can be in that given situation, altered to a positive ("B+") or negative ("B–") degree by the many factors that are outside of your control.

My practical experience with individuals from very diverse walks of life reinforces the fact that it is the same for everyone and this is why as a group, my high-performance clients are looking for a way to resolve this dilemma in their own mind. I have yet, in all of my years of experience, to find a situation where this simple equation does not apply. It has proven to be fundamental, universal, and infallible!

But how do you get around this problem of lost confidence? How do you maintain confidence in yourself when the results are far from what you had hoped they would be? The solution is simple enough in concept but it is not very easy to implement. It requires a level of "mental toughness" that is not the norm in the general population. You must adjust the personal yardstick by which you define progress and by which you measure your own effectiveness. Stated another way, you must change your *perspective* regarding the situation in front of you, and with this shift in mind-set, everything changes.

Think about this for a moment: If the results you ultimately achieve are most often outside of your direct personal control—because of the many "B" factors that can typically arise—choosing to define your confidence primarily by those results is the surest way to cause you to possess great confidence when things are going well, but see that confidence eroded when things are not going according to plan. As I mentioned previously, it is easy enough to have a positive mind-set when things are going well, but it is a very different situation when things are not! How do you get beyond this so that a string of poor results does not damage your confidence and corrupt your subsequent performances? Fundamentally, it involves a change in perspective.

Consider this question: What is the only thing that is truly 100 percent within your control, that is not dependent on any other factor? The answer of course is *you*, or more precisely, it is the commitment you make and the effort you invest to give your best every time you are called upon to perform. *You* are the only one who can choose to give less than your very best effort in the face of every challenge you take on.

Recognize that you are completely in control of the "A" factor in the Performance Equation but that you simply and fundamentally cannot control the "B" factors that might arise since by definition, they are outside of your control. Because you cannot control the "B" factors, you also cannot control the Results.

If you *choose* to honestly bring your best effort, to bring the strongest "A" game you are capable of and focus on executing to the best of your ability, there is nothing anyone else can do to prevent you from doing so. While it does not necessarily mean that you will achieve the result that you are seeking, you *are in control* of the quality of your personal performance and in so doing, the degree to which you optimize the likelihood of achieving the best result possible in that situation.

What do you think would happen to your confidence level if the personal yardstick by which you define progress and measure internal success is shifted to consider how well you stepped into the challenge when you were called upon to perform? By doing so, you prove to yourself on a consistent basis that you can be counted on to give your very best, no matter how great the challenge in front of you might be. As you repeat this way of thinking and its associated behaviors, your confidence will only become stronger because it is now defined in large measure by your effort and commitment as opposed to results that are actually outside of your direct control. Success should not be only about the results you achieve, it should be about the control, the personal commitment, and the effort you invest to give the very best you are capable of at all times.

Having said this, recognize that you and others will sometimes be disappointed about the outcome because results are indeed important and when you do not achieve the results you so desperately are working toward, it hurts. Results do indeed matter a great deal for the vast majority of professions.

I have never had someone approach me and say "I'd like to fail ... I want to be a loser ... I really hope that I finish last!" I am quite certain that in society, everyone *wants* to be successful. We all want to win because success is a tide that can lift all boats while failure has consequences that are often negative. Indeed, as we grow up (in school, on the sports field, in personal relationships, at work) our ability to generate results determines how we advance, the amount of money that we make, and even comes to define our reputation with others and indeed, our own self-esteem—the reputation that we have with ourselves. The lack of results may even cause us to lose our job! Unfortunately, the truth is that many people do not fundamentally believe that they can be successful while others genuinely do not know how to be—but everyone wants to win. It is part of our basic human nature and we all share this common goal or desire, no matter what our position in the company or on the team might be.

Now I would like to take a moment to address the concerns of the many managers and business owners who might be thinking, "What the heck is he talking about? This kind of thinking is going to create an army of workers who think that it is alright when they don't get the job done because they believe that it is all about the 'experience.' That's great. Now we are creating a built-in excuse for failure . . . the almighty "B" factor!"

Nothing could be further from the truth.

The need for goal-setting, accountability, timelines, performance targets, performance evaluations, and so on, remains an important part of the management process—for self and for others. Without short- and long-term goals to shoot for and a clearly defined process that we can use as a road map to help us get there, how will we know that we are making progress and that we continue to be headed in the right direction? Results are most definitely important, but we must clearly understand that results are a *consequence* of execution or process (performed by us and by others), almost always influenced by factors that are outside of our direct control.

 Results should be the goal of our performance, but when we are engaged in the performance, our focus should be directed to execution—the specific actions and tasks that are directly relevant to the performance itself. *This is the key.*

Our focus needs to be on the process of execution, in the moment, directed to the task in front of us because that is the mind-set that will help us to create the best result possible. To deliver our best performance, we must focus fully on execution and trust that the results will take care of themselves. But is this the way that high-performance people think? It turns out that it is when they are "on their game" and delivering their best performances, but not so when they are struggling or generating average performances. We will consider this point again a little later in this chapter.

This does not mean, however, that you simply ignore potential "B" factors. In order to be well prepared in advance of the event, you must consider the potential "B" factors that can and do commonly arise in the performance situation that you find yourself in. As part of this preparation, you must develop contingency plans to address specific "B" factors so that you will be ready to deal with and mitigate them if they do arise during the performance. But then the trick is to simply focus on execution. With this mind-set, you do not worry about "B" factors, you simply address them to the best of your ability if they do happen to arise. This is why high-performance people practice as much as they do, to be able to deal effectively with opportunities and challenges that are commonplace in a changing performance environment.

Such a philosophy or corporate culture demands a level of intellectual honesty on both sides of the table. From the workers' side, they must honestly evaluate whether they delivered their true, best performance. They must understand whether the issues that may have ultimately affected the outcome really were something outside of their control that could not have been foreseen or changed, or something that they failed to address that they could have in advance. They need to answer the question: "How could I personally have done it better?" From the managers' side, they must try to understand whether the employee did indeed execute their process at a high level and if so, accept that the lack of result may honestly have been due to something outside of their direct control—and act accordingly. They need to answer the question: "Can we make our process better and how can I help my employees work more effectively toward this process?" Unfortunately, sometimes the "system" takes the easy road and forces participants at all levels of the organization to sink or swim simply on the basis of results, without understanding or considering the reasons that led to that outcome.

Food for thought: As you climbed the corporate ladder, did you ever have a manager or boss who may have believed that you actually performed well but used you nonetheless as a scape-goat—who threw you under the bus—when the results were not what the company needed them to be? Did they do this even though something that was truly outside of your direct control, and could not have been foreseen, prevented you from accom-plishing your goal? Have you ever been that boss yourself?

If you take a moment and recognize that the results you so often seek are outside of your direct control, and then commit to simply bringing your best effort to the task (regardless of the out-come), your confidence in yourself will remain strong. This sense of confidence-in-self will then allow you to approach the ongoing and new challenges you face with greater calm and with a more directed focus on the *process* of that performance, rather than on its outcome. This mind-set and perspective will optimize your per-sonal performance.

The irony of this is, when you focus on the process of execution and commit to simply giving your best every time you are called upon to perform, the results most often take care of themselves and your performance generally ends up being the best you are capable of in that situation. Whether it leads to success in that moment is unknown because we do not yet know what "B" factors might impose themselves in that situation. One thing is certain, however: with this overriding mind-set you are more likely to be success-ful over the long term. This is the mind-set that successful, high-performance individuals are often able to exhibit in the face of adversity and ultimately, this is one of the main reasons why they come out on top in many competitive situations.

Each of us is probably aware of this from personal experience,

It is a fundamental truth that the more you focus on execution "in the moment" and the less you worry about the outcome (the results) while you are trying to achieve them, the better the results typically are.

but it is very difficult to retain the mental toughness that allows us to trust and implement this mind-set in a consistent way on a day-to-day basis. The *Rules of the Mental Road*© that we will discuss in the second section of this book will help to explain why this is so, and the A.C.T. Model© process that I will introduce in Chapter 12 will help you to understand how to begin to accomplish this shift in thinking using a simple, systematic, and self-directed process. For the moment though, I would like to revisit the question of how high-performance people direct their thoughts when they actually engage in their performances.

For a number of years, I have been using a simple questionnaire (the Dominant Motivators-Performance Profile, based on Atkinson's Achievement Motivation Theory) in my work with high-performance clients. This questionnaire seeks to understand how they actually deploy or direct their thoughts at the very moment that they step into their performance and begin to execute. I want to know what kind of thoughts their mind is typically focused on as they engage in their performance. I invite you to complete this questionnaire yourself. We will consider your responses later in this chapter, in comparison to the averages recorded within several populations of my high-performance clients.

Dominant Motivators—Performance Profile

Note: This version of the questionnaire targets athletes in competitive situations. Since it is not possible to include different versions of the questionnaire here, adapted to other groups, you will have to read into the questions somewhat and consider them from the point of view of the environment that you are thinking about.

   If the world you are interested in is something other than sport (for example, if you work in a corporate or business environment), when the questionnaire refers to competition, think of a major event or challenging situation in your own world. Circle the one response (a, b, or c) that best describes you and your thinking for each of the twenty questions that follow. There are no correct or incorrect answers since your response represents only how you see things. Be absolutely honest in your responses and let your answer reflect what you really think and feel.

PERFORMANCE PROFILE

1. Generally, my level of effort in any competition is:
    a. as high as necessary to get the job done
    b. always high
    c. often low on difficult tasks but high on easy tasks

2. I look forward to the next event and expect to:
    a. be recognized as a "winner"
    b. improve my personal and professional skills
    c. have to work harder than the last competition

3. When people tell me how well I performed (in spite of the outcome), I tend to:
    a. appreciate their acknowledgment
    b. look at it more objectively and analytically
    c. not believe them

4. When people try to explain why I did *not* perform well (in spite of the outcome), I tend to:
    a. get upset by their opinion
    b. analyze the truth of their statements
    c. believe them

5. When faced with new learning tasks, I tend to:

    a. not engage in tasks that risk mistakes

    b. take on tasks that may even risk making mistakes

    c. start easy or go for the most difficult task(s)

6. My focus in competition is:

    a. to finish as the "top dog"

    b. improving my personal performance

    c. to get through the competition without problems

7. I really feel that:

    a. winning is primary, my personal performance is secondary

    b. my personal performance is primary, winning is secondary

    c. playing it safe is primary, winning is secondary

8. More often than not, I:

    a. put pressure on myself to win

    b. think about executing with excellence

    c. think about not "screwing up" during competition

9. When I think about my performance goals, I generally think about:

    a. how I want things to end up at the end

    b. how I want things to occur during the competition

    c. what I want to avoid or don't want to see happen

10. Win or lose, my first thoughts are:

    a. I should have done better

    b. why didn't I do better

    c. you can't win them all

11. My persistence and intensity:

   a. remains high as long as I am successful

   b. remains high whether I win or lose

   c. remains high as long as I don't fail

12. I know and measure "success":

   a. by final outcome

   b. because it "felt" right

   c. because others tell me it was good

13. I know and measure "failure":

   a. by final outcome

   b. because it "didn't feel" right

   c. because others tell me where the problems are

14. When I win or lose, it is because of:

   a. my ability or lack of ability

   b. my effort or lack of effort

   c. other factors, including luck sometimes

15. Regardless of outcome, I tend to remain:

   a. optimistic and know people look at me as a champion

   b. optimistic and know that I will continue to improve

   c. pessimistic and wonder what people think of my ability

16. In general, I think:

   a. winning is exciting

   b. performing my job with excellence is exciting

   c. performing without incident is the first priority

17. **Before and during competition, I think about:**

    a. being recognized as a "winner"

    b. analysis, strategy, and technique

    c. not making mistakes

18. **I think that:**

    a. being positively compared to another competitor reflects my ability

    b. positive and negative comparisons to other competitors are to be used for personal improvement

    c. being negatively compared to another competitor shows my lack of ability

19. **If I fail in competition, I tend to:**

    a. work harder to regain my status as a real competitor

    b. think more about how to solve problems related to my personal performance

    c. lack focused effort in problem solving

20. **I tend to classify my personal performance as:**

    a. good enough to succeed but not at my potential

    b. high and approaching my potential

    c. not close to what I would wish for

To calculate your final scores:

- Total the number of "a" responses _____. Multiply by 5 = _____ %. (Motivation to Achieve Success—**MAS**)

- Total the number of "b" responses _____. Multiply by 5 = _____ %. (Motivation to Improve Performance—**MIP**)

- Total the number of "c" responses _____. Multiply by 5 = _____ %. (Motivation to Avoid Failure—**MAF**)

If you examine the research literature in the area of motivation, it is clear that, ultimately, human beings are fundamentally motivated by two key but opposite emotional drivers (Figure 1).

On one side of the ledger, we are motivated strongly by what we **fear**. Indeed, the things that we fear serve as powerful motivators to drive our thoughts, our behaviors, and our actions. This is why fear of failure is one of the most powerful motivators in the human spirit. Consider how the things that we fear—being rejected, being poor, being cold, being hungry, being alone and unloved, getting hurt, being laughed at and not with, being disrespected, and in its simplest form, "failing"—are powerful motivators that drive our behavior to try to avoid these situations at great cost. Did you know that according to major surveys in the general population, the fear of speaking in public outstrips the fear of death in the majority of people? Indeed, the fear of speaking in public is reported as being the predominant fear that people possess. Why might this be so? Perhaps it is because we fear that we will make fools of ourselves if we mess up and that others may think less of us as a result of such a poor, embarrassing performance.

Our psychological imperative to avoid failure pushes us to take deliberate action virtually every day.

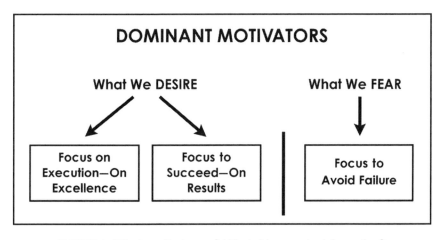

FIGURE 1. What motivates us? What drives us to take action?

On the other side of the ledger, we are also motivated strongly by the things that we **desire**: food, shelter, warmth, sex, security, to be loved, to have fun, to be respected, to feel wanted, to have money/stuff, to perform with excellence, to be seen as skilled and competent, to be successful—again in its simplest form; to win and to excel. These dominant motivators also drive our behaviors and directly influence the actions that we take to lead us in this success-oriented direction.

When we think about the performance world, we can subdivide the "desire" side of the ledger to include two different but related elements: the extrinsic reward of results and the intrinsic value of excellent performance itself. The extrinsic (or external) reward associated with a good result is easy to understand. This is the goal after all and when we accomplish the goal of a good result (whether it is in the work environment, in sport, in the recreational environment, or wherever), the result brings us reward: admiration; bragging rights; a sense of being the "alpha" in the group; money; fame; greater security; a step closer to a larger goal, and so on.

While we have all likely experienced the intrinsic (internal) value of an exceptional performance, this one is not so easy to define because the reward is not something that is generally tangible. It has more to do with the internal sense of well-being associated with a job well done, with having executed to the highest level that we are capable of. This feeling is separate and distinct from any reward that the outcome may generate. It is associated directly with our connection to and the quality of the execution itself, as perceived by ourselves.

Research tells us that extrinsic reward (such as money) can be a very powerful motivator early on but that all extrinsic motivators lose their potency with time. After a while, it requires a greater level of extrinsic reward to keep us fully motivated if that is the only driving force that moves us; the baseline shifts to where it now takes more of that extrinsic reward to motivate us to the same degree.

On the other hand, it seems that intrinsic reward is the most powerful driver or motivator for us humans. If we feel an intrinsic reward associated with some action, generally we will continue to engage in that action even if there is no tangible external reward (and maybe even if there is a personal cost) for our participation. This is in part what accounts for the millions of hours per year of time that are donated by people to charitable or mentoring causes all over the world. It is also worthy of remembering that if there is no intrinsic reward associated with what we are doing, extrinsic reward is not nearly as effective a motivator as we might think that it is.

We can use the analogy of a carrot and a stick to describe in a simple way how this works. A whack from behind with a stick or a pull from the front with a carrot has nothing to do with the donkey's internal, intrinsic motivation. The only result achieved by either of these approaches is that the donkey moves, but not of his own free will or choosing. The donkey responds to the external forces acting on it and moves only so long as he is forced or enticed to do so by external motivators (the stick and the carrot). As soon as those external motivators diminish in their importance, the donkey stops. A self-motivated person (or donkey) on the other hand, functions at a high level automatically and needs only occasional guidance and support to keep him headed in the right direction.

If **fear** and **desire** are indeed powerful motivators for all of us, how do successful high-performance athletes and occupational professionals actually think when they engage in their performances?

I want to share with you here some data that I believe you will find interesting. Table 1 summarizes the analysis of long-term data taken from the questionnaire (or one of its adapted versions) that you completed previously. I have pulled together a portion of the data from four different groups of clients with whom I have worked over the years to highlight how people who are thought of as being in the high-performance world actually think. In essence, this profile represents the allocation or deployment of their central processor—that is, how their brain inputs, stores, retrieves, and uses information—when they engage the main activity in which they perform. Note that the questionnaire that this data comes from was completed by each client before they began their program with me, so there is no influence possible due to my interaction with them. Before we look at the data however, allow me to give you some insight into who these people are:

Executives. This group pulls together data from 143 top-level executives and business owners/leaders (average age = 45.3 years). These individuals are "C"-suite level executives—part of the top executive team for their organization; They are CEOs, COOs, CFOs, and so on—with a few senior-level managers and sales professionals included in the mix.

Law/Fire. This group pulls together data from 33 command and supervisory officers (average age = 44.8 years) from various law enforcement and firefighting departments. These highly experienced individuals would be considered veterans of their law enforcement/firefighting professions.

Race Team Crew. This group pulls together data from 153 highly skilled professional open-wheel and stock car race team crew members (average age = 32.2 years). The group consists largely of individuals who go "over the wall" to service their team's race car during pit stops, with some senior team management and technical personnel included in the mix.

Racing Drivers. This group pulls together data from 119 high-level race car drivers (average age = 28.3 years). These individuals are drawn from the top levels of the motor racing world (Formula One, Indy cars, NASCAR, NHRA, sports cars, motorcycles, and so on), and would be considered among the best in the world at what they do.

Collectively, this aggregation of nearly 450 real-world individuals represents a group of highly proficient, experienced performers who are engaged in what most individuals would consider to be high-risk/high-demand professions. The numbers in Table 1 represent group averages relative to the three dominant motivators outlined previously (note that the last line in the table provides space for you to write in your scores from the questionnaire you completed earlier):

- **Execution (MIP).** An "in the moment" focus that is directed to the actions involved in the execution of the task in front of them; mentally connected to the act of execution as the performance unfolds; fully present, here and now! How much of their dominant thought is directed to the actions of the performance itself?

- **Results (MAS).** A focus that is directed primarily to the outcome of the act in which they are engaged; thoughts associated with the consequence of their actions if the results continue to evolve as they perceive them to be in this moment; they are in self-judgment mode, thinking about how well or how poorly they believe that they are doing while they are actually doing it. How much of their dominant thought is directed to the *outcome* of their performance (toward results)?

TABLE 1: DOMINANT MOTIVATORS
(average for each data set)

GROUP	# IN GROUP	EXECUTION (MIP)%	RESULTS (MAS)%	AVOID FAILURE (MAF)%
Executives	143	57.7	33.6	8.8
Law / Fire	33	61.1	30.3	8.6
Race Team Crew	153	58.2	29.5	12.3
Racing Drivers	119	55.0	32.8	12.2
Overall Average	448	58.0	31.6	10.5
Your Scores				

- **Avoid Failure (MAF).** A focus that is directed toward failure, toward the fear of messing up, and on the consequences of such failure; they are in full-blown worry mode, afraid that they will not be able to succeed, thinking about all the ways they could fail and worrying about what that failure might represent. How much of their dominant thought is directed toward not being able to get the job done successfully, toward a fear of failure?

Transpose your MIP, MAS, and MAF scores from the questionnaire you completed earlier to the last line of Table 1 and compare your scores against the group averages. How does your focus of attention differ from the high performers outlined in this table, or does the way that you deploy your focus of attention share some commonality with these other individuals?

I want to draw your attention to a couple of interesting points that we can take from this real-world profile. First, notice how consistent the average scores are across groups for each of the three dominant motivators. While there is some variability in the average scores, it does not really matter which of the groups we are looking at; they all essentially think the same way—regardless of the profession or job in which they are involved. Second, if you consider the "Overall Average" score in the next-to-last line of the table (based on 448 individuals), the data informs us that about 58 percent of their thought process seems to be directed toward execution while they are engaged in the act of executing, but that their thoughts are also preoccupied by other things (31.6 percent directed toward the outcome with regard to the task in which they are engaged, and 10.5 percent worried about failure).

Over the past four decades, this is what I have found to be the case based on measured data and from my extensive follow-up discussions with these individuals. This does indeed appear to be representative of the kind of thoughts that they often engage when they are out there "doing their thing." But are these thoughts what they should be?

What about you? Are your thoughts often directed to how well or how poorly you believe you are doing while you are engaged in the task at hand, or to nagging thoughts and fears that you will not be able to do it well enough and will fail?

Let us look at this data differently by aligning the kind of thinking measured in our groups of high-performance people to the variables of the "Performance Equation" we discussed earlier: **"A" x "B" = Results.**

The "A" variable seems straightforward enough—this kind of thinking puts us in the realm of "Execution" (MIP). When we are on our "A" game, we are fully connected to the action or act of execution itself, not focused on results or on the fear of messing up. We are calm, confident, and fully and exclusively focused on what we are doing at the moment that we are doing it. For our group of high performers in Table 1, in general it appears that 58 percent of their dominant thought is actually directed to the "A" in the equation—to the only thing that is truly 100 percent within their control.

The "Results" variable also seems straightforward enough—this kind of thinking aligns perfectly with the "Results" portion of our equation. Again, for our group of high performers, it seems that almost 32 percent of their dominant thought is preoccupied with the outcome of their performance rather than with the execution, *while they are in the process of executing* (MAS).

Finally, the "Avoid Failure" component (about 10 to 11 percent) aligns itself with both the "B" factor in the performance equation as well as the "Results" variable (MAF). In essence, we worry about the lack of results if we perceive that we are not doing very well, and worry about what the consequences of that failure might be if it continues the way that it seems to be going.

What is the impact of this kind of thinking if in fact it is representative of how people in the high-performance world actually think? If we consider our Performance Equation, the "A" variable is the only one over which we have direct control. We cannot control the "B" variable because by definition, this represents the many factors over which we have no direct control. Since we cannot control the "B" factors in the equation, we also cannot control the "Results." This is a fundamental, universal, and infallible truth.

If the above analysis is accurate, even high-performance people often seem to be preoccupied with negative and counterproductive thoughts when they are engaged in their performances, and only a little more than one-half (58 percent) of their cognitive (or central) processor is actually directed to the only part of the performance equation that is fully within their control. About 42 percent of their dominant thought appears to be directed toward things that have not even happened yet (outcomes) and over which they have no direct control (both the "B" factors and the Results).

 In my follow-up discussions with these individuals, I have come to understand that, although this might be the way they often think, it is **not** *how they think when they deliver their best performances.*

In fact, it appears that this is the way that they tend to think when they sabotage themselves, when an incorrect mind-set corrupts their ability to deliver the kind of superlative performances that they know they are capable of but only occasionally seem to be able to manifest. They are very interested in learning how to bring about the correct state of mind, on command. They recognize that if they manage to achieve this kind of mental control, they will deliver their best work more consistently, and automatically set aside the self-sabotaging mind-set that prevents them from doing so. I would like to go back, for just a moment, to the two most common requests I have been asked over the years by my high-performance clients:

- Show me how to keep my confidence high when things are not going well, and

- Show me how to focus more effectively, and when I lose my focus, how to get it back quickly.

If we consider the data drawn from my high-performance clients, we can see clearly why these two issues are the predominant ones in which they might be interested. Confidence is an important issue because we all tend to focus on results, and indeed we most often define our confidence around the results that we achieve, or fail to achieve. In fact, a third of our central processor appears to be preoccupied by a focus on results, and because we cannot control results we worry about whether or not we will ultimately achieve them. When things go poorly and the results are not what we had hoped for, we worry even more. As we worry more, our focus of attention shifts to the source of our worry rather than being on the task in front of us, and we become even less effective at delivering our best performance.

 This is why a ***correct focus,*** together with a strong sense of ***confidence*** in our own ability to deliver the best we are capable of, regardless of the challenge in front of us, is so fundamentally critical to the mind-set that allows us to deliver our highest quality performance.

CHAPTER 2

How We Mentally Process Information

I have a theory about the human mind. A brain is a lot like a computer. It will only take so many facts, and then it will go on overload and blow up.

—ERMA BOMBECK, HUMORIST

A computer will do what you tell it to do, but that may be much different from what you had in mind.

—JOSEPH WEIZENBAUM, AUTHOR & COMPUTER SCIENTIST

Before we dive into this topic, I want to set your mind at ease. It is not my intent here to undertake an in-depth consideration of the complex topics of neurophysiology or neuropsychology. While it is true that we understand a great deal about how the human brain functions, there is a great deal more that we do not understand.

Fortunately, we do not have to understand all the intricacies of these complex functions in order to know how to manage our thinking to improve personal performance. In this chapter we will discuss how human beings mentally process information, in the simplest of terms, so that you can better understand how central processing function affects performance. If you currently work in a business, sport, or occupational environment, you have likely been around long enough to know that how you think directly influences how you ultimately perform. You may not know exactly what to do about it yet, but you recognize that your mind-set is usually different when you perform at your best compared to when you perform poorly. You have also probably come to realize that the self-sabotaging behavior that you may sometimes be guilty of has its origin in mental thought. The information that we will cover in this chapter will help us to set the stage for the Rules of the Mental Road© that we will discuss later in the book, as well as our subsequent discussion of the A.C.T. Model© process.

In order to begin the discussion of how humans mentally process information, I would first like to introduce the concept of *cognitive function*. Cognitive function is an all-inclusive term that aggregates the complex mental processes that transform information that we acquire through our senses, encodes it so that it can be more effectively stored in our memory, and retrieves it for later use. Since human learning and performance invariably involves actively responding to environmental stimuli and organizing and/or reorganizing information that we acquire through this process, learning and performance always involve some kind of cognitive or mental activity.

We can use the analogy of the generic computer system to gain a clearer understanding of how these various cognitive functions might operate in the human mind (see Figure 2). The analogy, although simplistic, is a good one—even though no one has yet created a computer processor chip that even remotely approaches the complexity and power of the human mind! While the modern-day computer may be blazingly fast for many of its operations, it functions under rules that are amazingly simple: at the machine level, computer language fundamentally consists of only 0s and 1s. Let us start by looking briefly at the pieces and basic functions of the generic computer system.

The three basic functions at work within the typical computer system involve the processing of information during *input, storage,* and *retrieval* functions, coordinated in such a way as to accomplish specified tasks or solve problems. In our computer system example, we have both hardware (the physical pieces that make up the machine and its parts) and software components (the instructions that tell the different pieces how they are supposed to work together toward a common goal). The *input* devices (keyboard, mouse, camera, scanner, and so on) are designed to allow information that is acquired from the computer's external environment to be captured and translated into a form that the computer can understand, and then processed via the central processing unit— the CPU chip—that is the main brain of the computer.

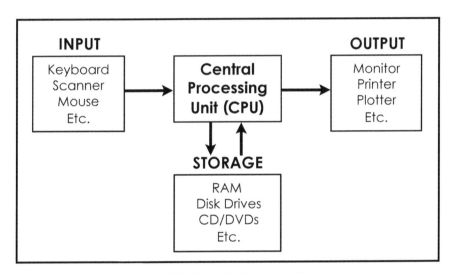

FIGURE 2. The Generic Computer System

The computer system possesses other physical structures that allow the information that has been input to be held for short periods of time while the brain is working with it—typically, a series of computer chips that allow for the digital storage and movement of information in short-term "random access memory" or RAM. The computer system is also capable of *storing* information that is deemed valuable in more permanent structures commonly referred to as "storage media," like floppy disks, flash drives, hard disks, CDs, DVDs, and so forth. Once the information is stored onto these more permanent storage media, it can be saved for a very long time and *retrieved* at will, similar to the stacks of reference materials stored in your local library that can be accessed with the right commands. On the retrieval side of the equation, the computer's CPU can tap these storage media for saved or archived material and use this information, in conjunction with any new information it acquires, to resolve tasks that it has been instructed to undertake. At the discretion of the user, the computer system can also output information via a variety of devices that translate processed data into a form that the user can then meaningfully interact with it, like monitors, printers, and plotters.

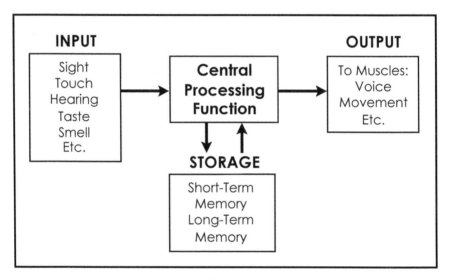

FIGURE 3. The Human Mind

Now let us compare the basic computer system described above with the human mind (Figure 3). On the *input* side of our mental processing function, the human mind acquires new information through our senses—the traditional five senses originally defined by Aristotle: vision, hearing, taste, touch, and smell, together with a number of more specialized but less commonly thought of classifications. Environmental information is then captured, translated, processed, and potentially stored in a form that the mind can understand (a series of chemical/electrical signals). However, we cannot point out the central processing unit as readily in the human mind as we can on the computer motherboard. In our computer system example, the CPU is a discrete structure—an integrated circuit chip—that can not only be identified, but can often be replaced if defective or upgraded to increase the systems performance! While we can point out the physical structures of the human brain and its associated central and peripheral nervous system components, we really cannot point to where the human *mind* is located. This is because the human mind is an abstract concept rather than a physical organ. Think of the human mind as a conceptual framework that operates via a *neural network*—a series of complex interconnections that occur in defined sequences throughout the brain's central structure, integrated with central and peripheral nervous system components that terminate at both the sensory and motor ends of the chain throughout the body. These sensory terminals allow us to capture and ultimately perceive information from our environment. The motor terminals allow us to activate muscles throughout our body to change our position with respect to that environment.

 On the *input* side of the equation, in order for learning to take place we must selectively attend to (that is, *focus* on) a source of information, often referred to as a "stimulus," while filtering out whatever other stimuli might be competing for our attention.

The selective filtering of information at this very first level of the input chain limits the volume of data that makes it into the conscious segment of our central processor. This adaptation has occurred because the sheer volume of information to which we are exposed in our environment would overwhelm our central processor's capacity to handle it, and we would simply become "overloaded" from a mental point of view. Have you ever felt overloaded or overwhelmed?

You might be asking yourself at this point, if this selective filtering process is real, what kind of examples would demonstrate this phenomenon? Consider the following:

Without looking at your watch, take your opposite hand and place it over the face of your watch, and keep it there. As you might expect, a great deal of research has been done to understand time and its management, and researchers have studied the issue to determine how often the average person looks at their watch on a daily basis.

> **How often would you guess the typical person consults his/her watch on a daily basis?**

Now, without removing your hand from the face of your watch (assuming you are wearing one), I would like you to take a few moments to answer the three following questions regarding the watch you are wearing:

1. What color is the face on your watch?

2. Are the markers that identify time in the form of roman numerals, regular numbers, dots, or dashes?

3. Are the markers different at 12, 3, 6, and 9 from the markers identifying other times?

Once you have decided on your answers, check your watch. How many of the questions did you get wrong? Would it surprise you to find out that nearly 40 percent of people who are asked these three simple questions get at least one of them wrong? And this occurs even if they have owned their watch for quite some time. Oh, and by the way, past research tells us that on average, the typical person will consult their watch just over 100 times per day. The truth is that today, that number might be quite different since a lot of young people do not even wear watches any longer; they use their mobile phones to monitor what time it is.

What this means is that if you have owned your watch for a year, you typically would have consulted your watch just over 36,500 times during this time period! How is it possible that more than a third of the people who undertake this little test get at least one of the questions wrong when we are talking about a patch of "real estate" that is only approximately the size of a 25-cent coin?

The simple answer is that when we consult our watch, we are usually looking to see what time it is, not what the watch looks like. Our mental *filter* is narrowly set and our goal within this action is specifically to determine the time. Unless you happen to be a watch aficionado and chose your watch *because* of its appearance, the chances are that you have not paid much attention to the intricacies of what the watch face looks like.

There are many examples of this kind of selective filtering of environmental information that is ongoing every day in our lives. When you first put on a pair of snug-fitting shoes or a piece of clothing, you sense the tight fit. Within minutes of wearing it though, the sensation of tightness gradually disappears and you no longer remain "aware" of it. When we first step into an environment that seems particularly loud, we notice the volume. If we persist in that environment however, the ambient noise soon fades into the background and we no longer remain conscious of how loud that environment might be. In a crowded restaurant bustling with activity, we often are not even aware of what is going on around us if we are engrossed in a particularly meaningful discussion with our dinner mate. You can think of this selective filtering process as a self-preservation mechanism that evolution has provided us with. It limits the amount of environmental stimuli that we process to a level that is manageable, protecting us from mental overload.

As with our physical computer system example, the human mind is also capable of *storing* information. We refer to this storage repository by the general term "memory" and the second component of the input process involves a very special form of memory that is reserved for recently received or registered information. This memory repository, often referred to as *short-term* memory, has a very limited storage capacity and does not last for very long. On top of this, data stored in short-term memory is very susceptible to interference or corruption. If we do not lock the information into a more enduring form of memory quickly (that is, into long-term memory), we will not be able to remember it beyond eighteen to twenty seconds. This transient "buffer" memory performs the function of temporarily holding recently received information just long enough for it to be analyzed and, if relevant, consolidated or encoded into longer-term memory. Working memory is then cleared to allow for the input of new data, and the process simply recycles itself on an ongoing basis. If the input is too rapid or the volume is too great, it can overload our central processor by overloading the short-term buffer memory. In so doing, the central nervous system protects us from acquiring too much irrelevant data.

When we encode and store information into long-term memory, it is usually organized in terms of our own individual past experience and prior knowledge. It is an active process where we give meaning to the recent experience and remember it in terms of this meaning. This is why two individuals can experience the same event and yet honestly manifest substantial differences between their accounts of the "facts" as they recall them. It is important to recognize that in most instances, we store in memory a *representation* of the information (what it means to us) and not a verbatim account of the information itself—the way an audiotape or video recorder might capture it. Memory storage and retrieval involves *reconstruction* of information or events rather than *reproduction*.

The third stage of the cognitive loop we have been describing involves the *retrieval* of information—the availability and utilization of previously stored or learned material. Often, recall involves a search and retrieval function for information that we might use in the process of problem solving and reasoning, or for analyzing and categorizing new material into memory. Memory can fail due simply to the passage of time or more often, as a result of interference from competing memory traces for the same space and association. The information may be unavailable because the data was not fully "registered" and logged in the first place, because it was badly consolidated, or because it was distorted when it was originally encoded and stored. As a result, our recall of the "facts" is corrupted.

In summary then, the cognitive process works something like this: In its simplest terms, in the input process, sensory information is selectively filtered such that only a limited amount of information is perceived and registered in our central processor. The information is then encoded in a limited capacity in short-term memory. In the storage process, the transient information in short-term memory that is important to us is processed and may undergo some form of rehearsal or repetition, often verbally, into more enduring long-term memory storage. The storage is further organized and the information is heavily influenced by its meaning in relation to our past experience and our belief or value systems. In the process of retrieval, memory is accessed for required information and either reorganized for output in a visible response or utilized in further internal cognitive activity. Our analysis of the information informs our response, as outlined in Figure 4.

It is important to recognize however, that in the simple "cognitive loop" illustrated in Figure 4, there is a bottleneck in the process.

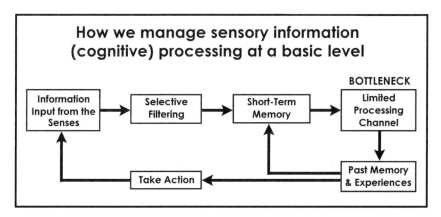

FIGURE 4. A Basic Cognitive Processing Model *(Adapted from Broadbent, 1971)*

The bottleneck exists because the active processing of information (active conscious thought) operates in a serial manner (one thought after another), rather than in a parallel fashion (many thoughts, all at the same time).

The analogy of a busy library has been used to further illustrate this concept (see Figure 5). Imagine that we have a busy library that employs only a single reference librarian. This individual is responsible for taking in, categorizing, cataloging, and placing into the stacks all of the books that make their way into the library, whether they are purchased or donated. Let us imagine that on a given day, a large number of donors come through the door to donate their books for permanent storage in the library. On one side of the desk we have the donors and their many books, and on the other side we have a number of empty library shelves waiting to be filled with books. The problem is, we only have one reference librarian.

FIGURE 5. The Reference Librarian Bottleneck

Coordinating all the activities involved in storing the donated books is important. Without coordination there would be disorganized chaos, and many of the books would be virtually impossible to retrieve since there would be no clear record of their location within the stacks. The librarian, however, can only process one book at a time and the categorizing/cataloguing function takes time. Because some of the book donors are impatient, they leave the line before their books are catalogued and their information is lost to the library. Other books, however, end up being processed—albeit in limited number—but they are correctly indexed and referenced for future availability and use. The librarian has processed as many books as he or she was able to in the time allotted but some of the books, due to sheer volume, never make it through into permanent storage.

When our mind is similarly challenged to retrieve, catalogue, and store sensory information, the inherent filtering system it has developed over time helps us to avoid a mental meltdown where we would be overloaded with so much information that we could not think straight. It also directly impacts our performance in ways that will become clear as we go along. Consideration of this cognitive processing model naturally leads us to a discussion of the conscious vs. unconscious mind.

The Conscious vs. Unconscious Mind

Many professionals in the world of psychology and psychiatry readily accept that the human mind can be functionally divided into two major areas that work in close harmony one with the other: the **conscious mind** and the **unconscious mind** (sometimes referred to as the nonconscious or subconscious mind). Assuming we accept this dichotomy of brain function, the conscious mind is a relatively straightforward entity to get our hands around. It is associated with conscious thinking, analyzing, the making of judgments and decisions, and it generally involves your inner voice speaking to you. Conscious thought is actually a slower (although such thoughts may only take a fraction of a second), more limited form of thought than most unconscious mental activities, because when we interact consciously with our environment, it generally involves a sequence of four steps:

1. sensory perception—what we perceive through our senses, limited in some way by our personal "filtering system,"

2. association—how we match up the information we perceive with our experiences and knowledge,

3. evaluation—what we believe the information means for us, and

4. decision—how we choose to respond to the situation, based on that meaning.

Whatever way you look at it, in the end you can do only one of two things with your conscious mind: you can react or respond with a conscious thought to something that is going on in your environment; or, you can generate a conscious thought that is independent and has nothing to do with your current environment or situation. For example, you might be trying to "connect the dots" by rationalizing what I have written here against your own experiences and understanding. In effect, you are reacting to something going on in your environment—the reading of this book. Alternatively, you might be daydreaming about what you will have at your next meal, thereby generating a thought that has absolutely nothing to do with the topic we are discussing. Both kinds of thoughts are possible, and at its most basic level, your conscious thoughts right now must necessarily fall into one of these two general categories. The beauty of this simple truth is that you can control this process completely!

The unconscious mind, however, is a much harder concept to wrap our hands around because we are not "conscious" of its operation and indeed, we are *not* in direct control of its processes. The unconscious mind regulates functions such as heart rate, respiration, hormonal levels in our blood—in fact, all of the processes that sustain human life. It also serves to coordinate all of our learned skills and complex actions, and is the driving force behind our emotions. As you sit reading this book, you are not consciously thinking about the very specific sequence of contractions of your heart muscle cells that keep blood moving through your cardiovascular system, or about regulating the contraction of your pulmonary diaphragm and the muscles that control the movement of your chest so that you can breathe, or about the processes necessary to repair damaged cells in your body. These functions are happening without any conscious thought on your part. They are certainly not happening randomly without any synchronized control, because if these processes unfolded in a truly random manner, none of us would be here! Something within us is controlling these and countless more functions throughout our body but it is not part of our conscious thought.

Now consider all the very complex skills that you have learned how to execute over your lifetime: walking, feeding yourself, hitting a baseball, playing a musical instrument, typing, driving an automobile, and so on. With practice, skills become automatic and they no longer require the conscious, deliberate thought that we once had to apply as we were learning to execute them. Yet, each of us has been able to learn to coordinate some very complex and sophisticated movements and actions without consciously thinking about the integration of all of the biological systems that have to work together to accomplish these tasks. Our unconscious mind operates "behind the scenes," and it should be obvious by now that it is many times more powerful than our conscious mind.

The simple metaphor of an iceberg (as illustrated in Figure 6) graphically describes this relationship between our conscious and unconscious mind. The part of the iceberg that is sticking up above the water line (our conscious mind) is very small compared to the mass of the iceberg that lies below the water line (our unconscious mind). The waterline that separates the two portions of the iceberg can serve to represent the boundary of our conscious awareness. In reality, there are no clear boundaries. For example, the simple process of catching a ball involves sensation, cognition, and reasoning processes without there being a clear separation between the single actions of choosing to catch the ball, seeing it, calculating its speed and direction, and coordinating the body movement necessary to grasp it. Then there is the question of emotions.

As hard as it may be to accept, it is a fact that we *cannot* directly control our emotions, although we can and often do try to control their expression to the outside world!

This basic truth is critical to understand because everyone realizes from experience how our emotions in the moment directly influence how we perform. In order to optimize our performance, one of the things that we try so hard to regulate is how we feel as we engage those challenging moments when we are called upon to perform. That is because emotions drive behavior and our behaviors directly influence how we perform. If all the other pieces that are outside of our control actually fall into place, it will also affect the results that we may be able to achieve in a given situation.

FIGURE 6. The Relationship Between the Conscious Mind and the Unconscious Mind

Over the years, I have encountered individuals who have challenged me on the assertion that we cannot control our emotions directly. They believed that they could *directly* control their emotions. Let us put this assertion to the test, then, to better understand what is really going on.

- Take just a moment and *please be sad now* . . . go ahead, be sad . . . so sad in fact that the sorrow you feel deep inside you causes you to sob uncontrollably with despair.

- Now, stop feeling this way and *please be happy,* so deliriously happy that the joy you feel in your heart lifts you up and you feel like you are walking on a cloud.

Okay, what happened?

If you truly could directly control your emotions, a directive such as the one I gave you should have allowed you to engage those emotions immediately, turning them "on" and feeling them deeply just by willing them to occur. But it does not happen that way, does it? In truth, the only way for you to become sad or happy in the way that I described is to think sad/happy thoughts, to fully engage your *conscious mind* in remembering past situations or events in your life that tore your heart in two or made you feel like you could soar like an eagle. The effect of those conscious thoughts gradually would cause the emotions of sadness or joy to build deep within you, feelings that are mediated by your unconscious mind. The cognitive processing loop we discussed earlier in this chapter informs us how our past experiences and memories are integrated with our ongoing conscious thoughts to drive any shift in emotion that we come to "feel."

It is clear from a great deal of solid research that cognitive processing does indeed occur outside the scope of our conscious awareness and that things that we might not be consciously aware of can and do influence other cognitive processes that our mind engages in, as well as our emotions and behavior. There is indeed a lot of mental activity going on that is not mediated or controlled by our conscious awareness. Fortunately, we do not have to understand the intricacies and complexity of the conscious and unconscious mind to understand how we can harness the power of our human mind to optimize our performance and stop sabotaging ourselves.

 I am going to simplify the landscape dramatically for our purposes here by outlining a couple of basic but powerful guiding principles that we will rely on as we move forward:

1. **The conscious mind looks at options (data) and makes decisions based upon our analysis, our experiences, and our belief/value system.** It is the part of our brain that we can think of as the data cruncher, analyzing the facts in front of us to consciously make sense of them. The conscious part of our mind is the rational, objective, discriminating faculty of the brain. Its role is to take in information from the environment, compare it with previous experiences, determine whether it is relevant or not, then finally make a decision. It is the part of our mind that we are in direct control of.

2. **The unconscious mind simply accepts what the conscious mind tells it, *whether it is true or not*, and then seeks to move us in the direction of our conscious belief.** Every single piece of information that the conscious mind accepts is then accepted by the unconscious mind as well. It is accepted as being true—as fact—*although it may or may not reflect reality*. I will say this again in another way—your unconscious mind does not dispute the accuracy or validity of the information you process within your conscious mind; it accepts it without debate as being fundamentally true, acts accordingly, and what is more significant, *you cannot control it*.

There you have it! These two fundamental principles will serve as the basis for our discussion of the *Rules of the Mental Road*© that begins in Chapter 5. For the moment, understand that the basic strategy we will build as we progress through this book will be to enlist the help of our conscious mind (by controlling our conscious thoughts—that is, by being the boss of our own mind) to in turn direct our unconscious mind to feel, behave, and perform in a certain way. As I have told my clients over the years, it really is that simple. It just is not that easy! However, there are two powerful mental tools that can help develop your ability to direct your unconscious mind more effectively. They are *imagery* and *concentration*. Let's look at imagery first.

CHAPTER 3

Imagery: The Language of the Mind

You can't depend on your eyes
when your imagination is out of focus.
—MARK TWAIN, AUTHOR & HUMORIST

I saw the angel in the marble and carved until I set him free.
—MICHELANGELO BUONARROTI, ARTIST, ARCHITECT, & ENGINEER

Imagination is more important than knowledge.
—ALBERT EINSTEIN, THEORETICAL PHYSICIST & AUTHOR

A picture is worth a thousand words.
—OLD AXIOM

I would like to begin this chapter by asking you to vividly imagine the scene that I describe in the following paragraph. Allow yourself to mentally step through this scene as if you were an active participant, fully connected to the actions being described.

Imagine that you are standing at your kitchen counter in front of the big cutting board where you chop up your fruits and vegetables. Find a sharp knife in your cutlery set and set it down on the edge of the cutting board. Walk over to your refrigerator and open the door. Reach down and pull open the drawer where you keep your fresh fruit. Pick up the largest, plumpest lemon you can find in the drawer and squeeze it gently, feeling just how ripe and juicy it is. Stand up, close the plastic drawer and the refrigerator door, and walk over to the cutting board. Put the lemon down on the board and pick up the sharp knife. Be careful to keep your fingers away from the sharp blade and slice through the lemon with a smooth stroke, cutting it in half. Smell the tart, citrusy smell that a freshly cut lemon produces. Take the sharp knife and again, paying attention to keep your fingers clear of the sharp blade, take one of the halves and cut it into two quarters. Put your knife down on the cutting board and take one of the quarters into your right hand. Bring it up to your face and inhale its tangy fragrance. Bring the quarter of that plump, juicy lemon up to your mouth, put it into your mouth, and bite down on it hard, sucking the tart, bitter juice into your mouth and down your throat . . .

How does that feel? Did you begin to salivate as your mind played through the mental images I described above? Did your face scrunch up a little bit and your jaws tighten as you imagined biting down and sucking on the sour lemon? The vast majority of people do. This little exercise highlights one of the basic truths about how the human mind works:

 The human mind does not differentiate between what is real and what is imagined!

How else could you explain that just imagining the scene with the lemon can cause the salivary glands in your mouth to explode and your jaw to clench at the mere thought of biting into that sour lemon? It is a revealing glimpse into how thoughts, framed as images in your conscious mind, can set into motion—via your unconscious mind—a complex series of physiological responses that lead you to engage a number of facial muscles and that stimulate the production of saliva, just as though you had really bitten into that bitter lemon. Not only is it interesting to recognize how effective this can be, but it can also provide insight into how we might use this basic truth to our advantage, rather than use it to sabotage ourselves.

People invariably think in pictures. In fact, there is not a single thought that we create in our mind that is not somehow associated with a mental image of some sort—and often, with a set of associated feelings as well. We often talk about seeing with our *mind's eye*. This simply means that when we imagine something in our mind, we generally see a picture of what we are thinking about, just as if we were looking at it through a camera lens or through our own eyes. Try thinking about something without "seeing it" in your mind's eye: your car, your desk at work, your favorite hat, and so on.

 Images that you process in your mind directly influence how you feel. These feelings in turn affect your behavior and these behaviors influence your personal performance in everything that you do.

To illustrate this fact, think back to a situation where you were watching a particularly sad, scary, or exciting movie. Your entire body responded to the images and feelings on the TV or movie screen as you watched the show and put yourself into the actors' shoes. Sometimes you felt tension or even fear in anticipation of what was to come, or relief when the tension-filled situation was resolved. Yet, you knew intellectually that these situations were not real, they were roles played out by actors following established scripts, often relying on crazy special effects. How is it that these "imagined scenes" can cause our body to respond in a very real way?

This reality in fact serves as the *mental computer program* that directs you to behave and then to perform in a manner that is consistent with the images in your mind and the feelings that you associate with those images.

It is important that you realize that the set of images and the beliefs that you create in your mind are *the reality* that truly exists for you.

I can illustrate this point further with another example. Imagine that I placed a wooden board flat on the floor in front of you. The board is six inches wide, perfectly stiff, and twenty-five feet long. If I asked you to walk the length of the board without touching the floor, would you be able to do it? It is likely that, not only would you be able to do it, but you could probably do it with your eyes closed or even do it backwards, if you put your mind to it. We have now established that you could easily walk the full length of this twenty-five-foot board when it is placed on the floor in front of you.

Now, imagine that I took that same twenty-five-foot board that is still six inches wide, perfectly stiff, and that you know you can walk along with ease when it is on the floor and suspended it between two buildings, 100 feet in the air. Even assuming there was no wind whatsoever and that we could ensure that the board remained perfectly rigid, do you believe that you could still walk the length of that board between the buildings with ease?

Likely not, and yet it is the same board with the same physical dimensions and features. Something in the mind of most individuals would stop them from even attempting to walk the length of that twenty-five-foot board. If they mustered the courage to attempt it, the fear and tension level that they would feel would be so great that many people would freeze up and not be able to move at all. But what has changed by lifting the board 100 feet into the air?

The only thing that has *truly* changed in this new situation is your belief or *perspective* regarding the specific challenge that you face in this situation. Because the consequences of falling off the board when it is suspended 100 feet off the ground are much more significant than when it is placed directly on the floor in front of you, you are no longer able to walk across that board with ease. As soon as you imagine all the nasty things that could happen, and perhaps even "see" yourself falling to the ground in your mind's eye, the tension level you feel rises dramatically and your ability to perform the task changes as well. This is a very important point to keep in mind, and the basic truth of the *dominant thought* principle that serves as the 4th *Rule of the Mental Road*© (see Chapter 8).

So often we create images of misfortune or failure in our mind and allow doubt to creep into our soul. Everyone has had these experiences. Often these thoughts are not based on likely outcomes or even on reality, yet they remain in our mind as powerful images of potential failure that influence our performance in a very negative way. If the mind can be influenced in a negative way, does it not stand to reason that we can also influence the mind in a positive way?

The good news is that we create our own set of mental images, and these images in our conscious mind directly influence—through the action of our unconscious mind—our feelings, the behaviors that flow from those emotions, and our ability to perform.

The bad news is that we create our own set of mental images in our conscious mind, and these images—through the actions of our unconscious mind—directly influence our feelings, the behaviors that flow from those emotions, and our ability to perform.

 The outcome depends completely on the kind of mental images that you put into your conscious mind, since the images you process there become the **dominant thoughts** that control how you feel, how you behave, and ultimately, how you perform.

A simple way to look at it is that the act of thinking involves three fundamental components:

1. The idea or the verbal component (you give it a label, a word to describe it).

2. The image or conceptual component (what you see in your mind's eye associated with that label).

3. The emotion or feeling component (what you feel or sense as result of that image).

The fact is that we mentally sow the seeds of our own success or self-destruction in many instances. Many times we allow destructive and counterproductive thoughts to dominate when we set about to perform, and we do not remind ourselves that a destructive image is just as powerful as a productive and constructive one. We do not think to control our mind to ensure that we process only positive and productive thoughts. What we do not realize is that images of failure or using negative self-talk such as "I just can't seem to ever get it right," create a condition for failure because this mind-set sabotages the relaxed physical actions that would allow your best performance to be expressed. In fact, a self-fulfilling prophecy of doom and gloom is now set into motion as your body attempts to fulfill the expectation created in your conscious mind. These thoughts and images become a blueprint for execution and performance, and we usually follow the influence of that blueprint, for good *or* for bad.

Now, let us consider some of the general principles and characteristics that define and give further clarification to this thing called *imagery*.

WHAT IS IMAGERY?

First, understand that the term *imagery* does not really describe the same thing as *visualization*. Imagery involves the creation of thoughts in our imagination that use all of the senses (sight, sound, feel, taste, and smell) to *influence* or *change* existing thoughts, feelings, or attitudes. Visualization—or "seeing with the mind's eye"—is a narrower concept since it only describes one part of the imagery process: the seeing part.

Think back to the moments you first saw a newborn child sleeping peacefully in his/her crib. Not only is it likely that you still carry a clear image of that experience, especially if it is your own child, but it is equally likely that this image is associated with a host of other feelings that might include warmth deep within your chest, joy, excitement, pride, love, and the like. You might even "remember" what he/she smelled like when they had just finished a bath and you dusted them in baby powder.

Mental imagery for performance is not daydreaming about the great athlete, business leader, musician, racer, or actor that you would like to be. Nor is it wishful thinking about how you would like to perform (how successful you might be) during a particular event. It is a learned skill that requires effort, quality practice, and focus to master. You can think of imagery as "mental holograms" that link your mind to all parts of your body involved in producing a particular performance.

Who of us has not imagined themselves to be the best in the world at some activity? The question is whether you then attempted to reproduce the mind-set and the behaviors that are consistent with the image you created in your mind. When you do this successfully, you are mentally programming yourself to perform like a champion. Fortunately, as children we possess a natural ability to use such imagery skills. Unfortunately, as we grow into adulthood, we often let these important skills slip away, or when we do use them, we use them to work against our own success by constantly sabotaging our performance because we adopt the wrong kind of mind-set!

How Does Imagery Work?

In essence, images and feelings that are created in your mind activate your nervous system in much the same way that it is activated when you are experiencing the actual event. It is almost like a mind-body rehearsal for the activity that is about to occur.

I am going to present an exercise here (see the Pendulum Exercise) that I hope will be effective in demonstrating in a practical way how mental imagery translates directly into a physiological response and action. I would like to take a moment beforehand, however, to put this task into context.

When I undertake this exercise with my clients in person or with groups of people in a live setting such as a seminar or workshop, approximately 85 to 90 percent of the participants typically demonstrate the response that is expected. For the 10 to 15 percent of participants who do not get movement of the pendulum, it is almost always associated with one of two reasons:

1. First and most commonly, they misunderstand the initial instructions and believe that they are supposed to prevent the pendulum from moving, regardless of the instructions I might subsequently give. When I tell them initially that I do not want them to consciously move the pendulum, they interpret this statement as a directive to keep the pendulum still and prevent it from moving. When this is their dominant thought, the pendulum usually remains somewhat still.

2. Second, individuals who tend to demonstrate an unusually tight control of their emotions generally do not give themselves over easily to the imagery I describe. They resist the influence of the suggested imagery and again, the pendulum does not move very much, if at all.

As such, I am not certain if this exercise will work as well in this format (that is, self-directed, from a book) as it does when I undertake it in person, but I encourage you to try it nonetheless and see where it leads. You may even want to try it with someone else, where you give the instructions and observe the response as executed by them, or in turn have them read the instructions out loud to you so you can focus on the imagery associated with the exercise. The outcome of this exercise invariably becomes an eye-opening—if not a little spooky—experience that has allowed many people to "connect the dots" and gain greater clarity as to how the way that they think directly influences how they perform. If it does not work for you, recognize that this sometimes is the case for various reasons, and I encourage you not to disregard it as being valid. Let us turn our attention now to the specific exercise that I've been discussing.

The Pendulum Exercise

I do not want you to try to move the object or pendulum on purpose during this exercise, but if movement does start to occur, *allow it to move freely.* The object of the exercise is not to keep the pendulum still, nor is it to move it on purpose. It is simply to see what impact powerful imagery can have on the way that our body responds to such mental images. Have someone read the instructions out loud for you, if you prefer.

Start by examining the illustration presented in Figure 7. Then take a lightweight string about 12 inches (30 centimeters) long and

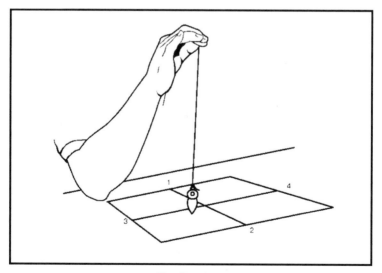

FIGURE 7. The Pendulum Exercise

tie a metal washer, a heavy paper clip, or a fishing weight to one end of it. Grasp the other end of the string between the thumb and forefinger of your dominant hand, with your elbow resting comfortably on the table. Center the hanging pendulum and suspend it just above the intersection of two lines that you have drawn on a piece of paper, as shown in the diagram. With your eyes open and focused on the object, I want you to *imagine* that there is a powerful cone-shaped magnet positioned under the table, directly below the point of intersection of the two lines. This magnet exerts such force on the metal pendulum that it keeps it *perfectly still*, pulling on it through the table right at the crosshairs of the two lines. The image of the pendulum being perfectly still is crystal clear in your mind's eye . . .

Now, imagine that the magnet is withdrawn from its position immediately beneath the intersection of the two lines. Picture in your mind's eye what the pendulum would look like if it started to ever so slowly swing from side to side, beginning to move gently between the numbers 3 and 4 that you have drawn on the piece of paper. Vividly imagine it happening in your mind's eye . . .

Continue to imagine what the pendulum would look like as it *gains momentum, increasing* its side-to-side movement more and more. Still using your mind's eye, imagine the pendulum continuing to swing back and forth—moving with such amplitude and momentum that it begins to reach out toward the edges of the page with each passing swing. See the pendulum moving in your mind's eye, and imagine what it would *feel* like if it responded the way that you imagine it, according to the clear, vivid picture in your mind of it swinging back and forth.

Now, imagine that the magnet was reinserted just below the intersection of the two lines and that it begins to exert yet again its force on the head of the pendulum. Picture the pendulum slowing down, being pulled back to the center of the two intersecting lines because of the powerful attraction of the magnet through the table. Imagine how it would *feel* if the pendulum were to slow down, reducing its travel, diminishing its movement, until it came to rest quietly right over the intersection of the two lines . . . the magnet pulling on it so powerfully that you must keep a firm grip on the string or it might slip through your fingers . . . perfectly still, with no movement whatsoever . . .

With practice and a relaxed "touch," most individuals are able to experience movement of the pendulum as they begin to imagine it moving, and then experience a quieting of the pendulum's movement as they imagine the placement of the magnet and its effect. With mental training, this ability gets stronger, and you can make the pendulum move in whatever direction that you can imagine, simply by vividly focusing your mind on the images, and feelings of the action you wish to see occur.

But why does the pendulum typically move in this manner?

It is a scientific fact that your brain is constantly transmitting electrical impulses to your muscles when you execute any physical action, and we know that this kind of mental activity is even occurring at rest. We refer to the activation of muscle at rest as *muscle tone,* and it is a property of muscle cells that is universal in all species.

 It is also a fact that the same electrical impulses, but at a lower level of intensity, are also being transmitted down the nerves to your muscles when you just *think* about executing the action.

In fact, if we placed small recording electrodes for muscle activity on the muscles of your shoulder, upper arm, and your forearm, we would see the same sequence of electrical signals directed to the same muscle groups, whether you are consciously and deliberately controlling the movement of your arm to slowly swing the pendulum in the desired way, or simply thinking about moving it. The difference lies in the intensity of the signals and not where they are directed. When you are just thinking about or imagining it, the same muscle groups are being activated, but it is like the "volume"

is turned down. It is not a conscious directive to move the pendulum; it is an unconscious response to the dominant images in your mind that paint the picture of the pendulum moving as you vividly imagine it.

The images and thoughts you create in your mind during the exercise with the pendulum are transferred as electrical signals to the muscles of the hand, arm, shoulder, and so on, but at a reduced intensity.

Imagery is kind of like using an electrical dimmer switch in your brain—similar to the ones you might have in your house to adjust the intensity of a light—in order to turn down the intensity of the electrical signals that are being sent to your muscles. As strange as it may sound, simply by imagining the movement of the pendulum in our example, you create a set of mental impulses or commands in your brain that are transmitted down the nerves to the muscles that cause the movement of your arm, but you are not consciously aware of it because it is mediated by your unconscious mind.

This is the same mechanism that explains why imagining that we are biting into a lemon causes us to salivate, why thinking sad thoughts often causes us to cry, and why watching a scary movie causes our heart to race and our muscles to tense. Consider the significance of this fact for a moment—how thoughts that you formulate in your mind actually trigger very real physical responses in your body as a direct consequence of what you are thinking.

What Is Negative Imagery?

Negative imagery involves the creation of thoughts and pictures in your mind that focus on images of disaster or failure. The more you try to purposefully avoid this negative image, the more energy and strength the negative image gains. The more you try not to think about it, the more it sticks in your consciousness and bounces around like an annoying tune that you simply cannot get out of your head!

Have you ever constantly reminded yourself not to get nervous in the lead-up to a big event, only to become very nervous and not be able to relax? Have you ever admonished yourself not to get upset or angry about something that may have happened, only to become more and more upset as you think about it more? Have you ever reminded yourself with passion not to slice when preparing to drive from the tee on the golf course, only to execute a perfect slice—just the way you pictured it in your mind. The reason that this often occurs is that by allowing yourself to think this way, you implant a set of negative images and feelings in your mind that serve as the dominant and persistent thought that directly affects your feelings, your behavior, and your performance, in a negative way. Remember, the pendulum simply moves in the manner that you imagine it. It does not debate your choice of direction!

The Basic Approaches to and Different Types of Imagery

We typically employ two different strategies when we use mental imagery to analyze and improve personal performance. They are often referred to as: 1) *view mode* and 2) *do mode.*

In view mode, you "see" images in your mind and you observe your performance as if you were viewing yourself on a movie screen, taking what might be thought of as a third-person view of the action going on at the time of your performance. In do mode, you are an integral part of the movie that is presented in your mind—acting out the different actions in your mind's eye, seeing and feeling it from the inside; you are engaged in the execution of the action, as you would experience it in real time.

Internal imagery (do mode) generally has a stronger influence on performance than external imagery (view mode) does for most people, since all of the senses are operating to influence your actions, compared to the use of only one sense that is active in view mode—the visual one. In either case, it is desirable to use both external and internal methods of imagery to analyze and enhance your performance. When you execute a particularly good performance, try to describe for yourself what it *looked like* and how it *felt*. Examine and analyze your performance in both view and do mode to better understand the imagery characteristics associated with excellence when you do your *best* work. That way, you can begin to model excellence by establishing the mind-set and the directed mental skills that will help you to perform at the highest level you are capable of, on command.

There are fundamentally two types of imagery that can be used to improve performance. These have often been referred to as *psychological imagery* and *performance pre-/replay*.

Psychological Imagery

This type of imagery is typically used to control pre-event anxiety, frustration, self-doubt, and other mind-set variables that influence your readiness to perform like a virtuoso or champion. It may also focus on generating controlled energy so that you are more alert, aware, and sensitive to the environment around you, without being over the top in terms of mental activation level. Anxiety, most often caused by self-doubt or an overriding fear of failure, is one of the most common problems that we all face when we engage challenging performances of any kind. When we are anxious, this anxiety leads to physical tension and an inappropriate mental focus, which in turn makes it simply impossible to deliver our best work. So how might you use psychological imagery to help resolve this conflict and improve your personal performance?

You might start by imagining different possible problems or challenges (the "B" factors that are out of your control discussed in Chapter 1) that can and often do happen during the course of a personal performance in which you might be engaged: problems with the public address system or lights; poor weather conditions; good and bad lies; uncooperative participants; distractions, and so on. Then, imagine how you think and behave as you correctly adjust and take advantage of any situation. Always finish this imagery by seeing and feeling the successful application of your skills in spite of the adverse conditions. This application of imagery may use some or all of the senses (sight, hearing, touch, taste, and smell) to recall and re-experience mood-states that are associated with a performance delivered with personal excellence in these types of challenging conditions.

In do mode, you would use as many of your senses as possible to experience a positive and productive condition that reflects your image of how someone at the top of their game would think and feel in that same situation. This could involve an increase in self-confidence, a calming mind-set, or any number of behavioral qualities that influence you to release your natural talents and abilities and express them within the performance in which you are engaged, regardless of the challenges that you face. In view mode, you might see yourself possessing the qualities that you would need in order to maximize your readiness to perform with personal excellence, regardless of how difficult the situation is and how well or poorly things are going. This imagery would entail seeing yourself this way as if you were watching a movie, with you being the main actor.

But it is important to realize that different qualities are needed for different individuals. Not everyone requires a calming influence before their big performance; some people need to energize to a more "activated" level to get the most from themselves. Other individuals must find a sense of internal quiet within themselves to perform at their best. The process to understand what level of arousal is best for each individual is discussed later in the book in the chapter that deals with the A.C.T. Model© process. Suffice it to say, the variety of images and qualities that encourage best-ever performances are as numerous as there are performers. Even though there are some common traits to this mental zone of excellence, this is not a case where "one size fits all"!

Performance Imagery

This is the inner playback mechanism of the mind. This type of imagery allows you to pre-play in your mind the images and feelings associated with excellence in execution as you prepare to undertake some performance. It can also allow you to play back (replay) in your mind's eye some event in your past as though you had captured the event on video with all the sights, sounds, and smells of the real situation. If your performance in the event was satisfactory, then you may simply review that performance giving yourself the implicit instruction that you want more of the same to occur. This type of imagery has less to do with the general mind-set that you possess as an underlying feature of your performance and more to do with the actual skills required and delivered within the execution of the task in which you are engaged.

If you are dissatisfied with your performance, a mental replay of the event can provide you with the opportunity to discover exactly what is in need of improvement. Once you have settled on a possible reason for a poor performance, you can replay the scene or the event with the new modifications you need to implement to change your mental images and your performance to the desired outcome.

Whenever you use performance imagery to direct your mind-set toward excellence, you are in effect programming your mind and body for future performances that will be delivered with a greater degree of excellence. It is a fact that excellence in perform-ance can be modeled, and if you work at correctly modeling excel-lence, you *will* more consistently be able to perform with personal excellence—on command. The pendulum exercise helps us to understand how this might come about. Keep in mind, though, that this does not guarantee that the result you are hoping for will automatically be generated, because we simply do not know what the "B" factors might be and how they will affect the outcome.

When Can Mental Imagery Be Utilized Effectively?

Mental imagery can be effective from the first instance that we are exposed to a new situation, or a new skill is learned to the highest levels of performance. The goal of imagery training at different stages of the skill development process can, however, be different.

A performance pre-play/replay type of imagery is typically more effective when the performer has a reasonably good understanding of, and some degree of practice in, the actual skill that he/she is trying to perfect. If you have little or no understanding of the technique that you are trying to perfect—say with a golf swing or a tennis serve, for example—you will likely not benefit to as great a degree from performance imagery training. In fact, you could even be impeding your ability to learn the skill because you are mentally rehearsing that skill without really understanding what you need to do to improve your performance. Your mental images may be all over the map—and incorrect—from a technique point of view.

To examine this concept further, consider a typical scenario that unfolds on playgrounds throughout the country virtually every day; that of a novice baseball player just learning how to hit the ball with a bat. Even the youngest child has some idea of what the outcome of the skill is supposed to look like because they have watched adults or other children execute the skill with some success. They generally understand that the ball is supposed to be struck with the bat and it is supposed to take off. Typically the farther, the better! The pressure is on in their own mind to perform because kids (and even adults) automatically tend to measure their own self-worth by the outcome of their performance. Often, this self-judgment is reinforced by the behavior and comments of some of the adults involved, and not always appropriately so.

When such a complex batting skill is first being acquired, not all children easily master the motor control needed to strike a ball with an object. For some, it may take some time to even make contact with the ball. Here are two possible scenarios that could describe, at the extremes of the continuum, the circumstances of such a learning experience:

1. The parent or coach becomes progressively more frustrated that the child is not hitting the ball, and the increased frustration is expressed by verbal commands that become more abrupt or

long-winded, and are delivered with a harsher tone of voice. The focus of the adult's feedback becomes overly technical and centers on an elbow here, a knee there, a hip elsewhere. Perhaps the catcalls by other children begin, and the young player's performance crumbles!

2. The parent or coach uses feedback that focuses the child's mind on the relaxed rhythm of the swing and on the fun challenge of *working at* making contact with the ball. Progress is realized by first having the child just tap the ball with an easy motion and little backswing, and proceeds in gradual increments that allow a greater level of success. *Effort* and the *willingness to try* are verbally rewarded and reinforced rather than only the outcome of the attempt, whether or not or how far the ball flies. The young player comes away with a better experience that he/she can build on during their next attempt "at bat."

I have used this example because it blends the two elements of imagery: psychological imagery and performance pre-play/replay. The two scenarios are offered only to provide a backdrop to briefly consider the performance consequences that could result in response to the type of imagery that very likely would be produced in the child's mind in these situations.

In the first scenario, the sense of failure that the child may feel at never properly "connecting" with the ball (fueled by comments like "Get out there and whack that ball a mile!" and the real or imagined frustration shown by the parent or coach, catcalls by peers, and so forth) leads to emotional anxiety and imagery that is associated with not being able to get the job done. The imagery associated with this mind-set induces fear of failure, tense movements, poor rhythm and timing. This failure-dominated imagery naturally leads to physical tension—remember the pendulum— and this makes the task of hitting the ball with a relaxed swing that much more difficult because of an overriding fear that he/she will not be able to do so.

Does it mean that in these pressure situations, the child will not be able to hit the ball? It should be obvious that this is not necessarily the case. But the physical reactions that are generated by the negative imagery created in the child's mind in response to this situation will make it more difficult for them to be successful in executing the task properly. The poor kid cannot wait for his/her turn to be over so that he/she can extricate themselves from this pressure-filled, failure-focused situation. For many children, repeated exposure to this type of pressure leads them not to even want to play anymore, and when they do try, they often predetermine the outcome of any attempt by sabotaging their performance every time: "See, I told you I couldn't do it!" We will consider the reason for this later in the book as we discuss the seven key *Rules of the Mental Road©*.

How is the second scenario different?

In the second scenario, input or feedback from the coach or parent serves to implant dominant thoughts into the child's mind that are associated with being relaxed, having fun, playing with an easy rhythm and flow to their movements, and so on. These underlying feelings and behaviors would increase the likelihood that the child would more effectively learn the skill from a technical point of view, because this is the mind-set that predisposes them to more easily acquire the nervous system training (often called "neural grooving") that will lead them to perfect the skill over time.

Moreover, because the focus of the feedback and its associated imagery is directed to the *effort* they put into the task and their willingness to try rather than the outcome of the attempt, the consequences from the child's point of view are not dire but in fact are rewarding, so long as they give it their all. When effort is reinforced and rewarded, especially in the early stages of skill acquisition, kids are more than happy to come back and try again, and with practice and some effective technical coaching (enlisting the process of performance pre-play/replay), most everyone can continue to develop their skills and improve their performance.

Think back to the first time you yourself tried to learn a complex physical skill, even as an adult. What mind-set predisposed you to learning that skill more effectively? It is likely that a relaxed, focused, and eager mental predisposition would help you to learn the skill more easily. What do you think the prospects of acquiring that skill would be, however, if you were physically tense, tentative, and worried excessively that you would not be able to learn the skill or that you might come across as an "uncoordinated klutz" to others who might be watching you? Now transpose these concepts to a situation that you might encounter in your job and within the performances that you or one of your business colleagues are called upon to execute: on a sales call, during a formal presentation, analyzing a difficult situation, reacting to a challenging management function, and so on.

When a young athlete first attempts to acquire a complex skill, the focus of his mental preparation should be oriented toward psychological imagery, with a focus on being relaxed, loose, and having fun. This is something that he can usually get his mind around fairly easily without yet fully understanding what the technical aspects of the skill might be. As his technical proficiency improves, training typically responds well to a mix of psychological imagery and a progressive introduction of performance imagery. As his skill level improves, the mentor or coach can cue him to gradual improvements in technique when these are demonstrated and when he is successful in executing the task correctly, and encourage him to describe how he thinks it looked and how it felt doing the task that way. The idea is to focus on the *look* and *feel* of what success or "excellence" is like. As performers become more accomplished and skillful, both performance imagery and psychological imagery are used extensively.

Are There Any Potential Pitfalls to Using Imagery?

You should be aware that there are potential pitfalls when you use performance imagery in particular to supplement actual practice.

The first pitfall relates to the quality or "accuracy" of the imagery you associate in your mind with the physical perform-ance. Let us assume for the sake of discussion that you are working on the execution of your golf swing, but do not really have a good understanding of what that swing *should* look like from a technical or biomechanical point of view. Whether your imagery is faulty or not, your body will attempt to replicate the physical actions that derive from that imagery. This is the reason why I mentioned previ-ously that performance imagery is not usually as effective—and may even be counterproductive—in the early phase of learning a new physical skill. Once you have a better understanding of the correct technique involved, then performance imagery can have a pronounced beneficial effect.

A less obvious pitfall involves using performance imagery asso-ciated with the correct technical execution of a skill, but only under ideal conditions. I can illustrate what I mean by this with the fol-lowing example, again related to the golf swing.

Let us now assume that your skill level is good and that you have a good sense of what technique is required when making the perfect tee shot. In your mental practice (imagery training), you replay the look and feel of what you consider the perfect shot from the tee, and you do this frequently. You mentally "groove" the per-fect tee shot! Then you find yourself out on the course and have to dig a shot out of a bunker with a short iron. If the only shot you have mentally practiced is the tee shot, it will be difficult for you to adapt your shot to the different technical profile required for a bunker shot.

The imagery that you use needs to be related to the *process* of the task you are executing, but it is also important that you allow for spontaneity in your mental imagery. Do not make the mistake of playing and replaying your actions under a set of constant con-ditions. Some individuals imagine the same ideal situation each time, and if you run only one scenario in your mind, you may be influenced to perform according to the limiting neural imprint set in your mind by the repetition of that one dominant program. If you do this, you will not be as well prepared to be dynamic and adaptable as you accommodate the variety of conditions and situations that confront you during such actions. Instead, using the golf example again, picture hitting the ball correctly from different lies, on the fairway or in the rough, in the sand trap, and so forth. In each case, build an imagery library that reflects excellence in execution, regardless of the situation. The same thing applies to the mentor or coach who is trying to direct the use of imagery by someone trying to perform complex skills. As their proficiency improves, introduce variations in the imagery model that they can practice based upon the differing demands inherent in performing these tasks in the real world.

Mentally rehearse situations that you may often find are problematic, that demand versatility and adaptability in how you respond to them, and that challenge your skills to the fullest. The more you see yourself in these difficult situations and the more you imagine yourself as you perform successfully in dealing with these challenges, the more you establish an unconscious mind-set that facilitates your correct performance when these situations arise down the road.

When the imagery you develop is correct and clear, your potential to push the limits of your skills and capabilities is increased. Under these circumstances, it can help to exaggerate the images to some degree. For example, a golfer might mentally see the cup as being twelve inches in diameter, making it impossible not to drop their putt into the center of the cup. They can slow the action of the putt down so they can increase the precision of their shot. Once their imagination is under control, they can start to execute the action with precision and confidence.

When doing this kind of mental training, you should practice only as long as you can maintain appropriate concentration on the images and feelings associated with correct execution. For some individuals this may only mean a few minutes at a time, while others can practice for a longer time period as they become more proficient. If you continue to practice while distracted and bored, you will simply be training yourself to be distracted and to lose focus.

Imagery training under these circumstances would be detrimental to performance. On the other hand, if you mentally rehearse situations where the likelihood of becoming fatigued or bored is high and you use it to work on maintaining the correct energy level and the appropriate focus, you are in effect programming your mind to perform better in these situations. It depends on how you use the imagined situation.

How Can You Enhance Your Ability to Use Imagery?

Practice does *not* make perfect.
Practice only makes permanent.

Only perfect practice makes perfect.

- Skill and efficiency increase with *quality* practice. Fortunately, our ability to use and benefit from imagery training is a learned skill. With more quality practice you will become adept at using more and more of the five senses in your imagery. This will ensure a greater positive influence on your performance.

- Create a receptive and comfortable atmosphere. Usually this means a relaxed frame of mind should be part of the ideal mental setup to begin imagery. All effective mental training protocols used today begin with some form of relaxation procedure prior to the actual mental training.

- Use all your senses. When you use more of your senses than just vision, you are stimulating more neural connections and associations in your mind. These connections can enhance specific performance.

- Music can increase the effects of imagery. Many individuals find it easier to relax and are more receptive to meditative imagery with background music. Some forms of music facilitate changes in your brain wave pattern that allows this relaxed receptivity to images that enhance your performance.

- Imagery associated with emotion makes the image's influence more powerful. Integrating an emotion into an image makes it more dominant and effective. In fact, stronger emotions tend to subordinate or eliminate weaker ones. Using strong emotions produces a more powerful impact than just imagining the desired performance or mind-set.

THE FOUR STAGES OF LEARNING

There are many researchers who have suggested different models that represent the various "stages of learning" that occur when we develop a complex skill in any task—progressing from a beginner level to that of expert. Advocates of *learning theory* have outlined four basic stages that help us understand how imagery training can influence each stage of the skill-learning process and why (see Figure 8).

1. Unconscious Incompetence

The first stage in the learning of a new skill has been described by the phrase *unconscious incompetence.* At this stage of skill development, we do not even know what it is that we are supposed to know! We are not yet aware (not conscious) of the various technical elements of the skill we are seeking to perfect and as a result, we are generally not very good at it yet (incompetent). Again, think back to your own experiences. When you first tried to learn a complex new skill such as driving an automobile, for example, you were not even sure of all the things that you had to be aware of and do behind the wheel, and you may even have felt a little overwhelmed trying to keep everything straight that you knew you had to consider. How difficult was it to keep the speed consistent, especially on the highway, without constantly having to check the speedometer and adjust. How much easier is it now that you have become a presumably proficient driver?

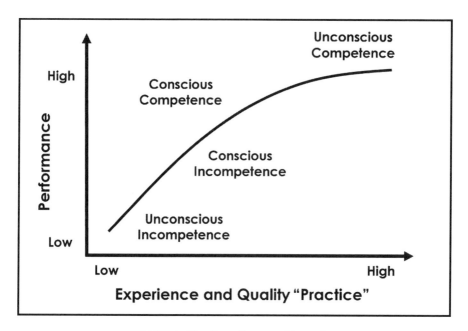

FIGURE 8. The Four Stages of Learning

2. Conscious Incompetence

Stage two in the learning model is best described by the phrase *conscious incompetence*. At this stage of skill learning, we begin to realize (become conscious of) what it is that we have to master, but have not yet acquired the necessary skills to perform the task correctly every time (relatively incompetent). We know what we need to do as time (and practice) goes on, but we just cannot do it consistently—yet.

3. Conscious Competence

The third stage in the learning of a new complex skill is defined by the phrase *conscious competence*. We now are much more aware (conscious) of the skills required to perform at a high level and be competitive, and we can frequently demonstrate these skills (we have become relatively competent).

4. Unconscious Competence

The fourth and final stage in the learning curve is defined by the phrase *unconscious competence*. At this stage of skill level, we experience moments during the execution of a task where we become totally absorbed in the action itself (unconscious) and perform effortlessly with personal excellence (competent) in many instances. Absolute focus on the "now" serves to eliminate all other thoughts and feelings that are not pertinent to what is happening right now, moment by moment. Some individuals have described these moments of excellence in which time seemed to slow down. They felt that they were well ahead of the action, and some have even experienced the sensation of being able to control the outcome (even though, in actuality, they cannot). These situations of excellence are often described as being "in the zone" or on "autopilot"—when you feel comfortable, focused, and energized all at the same time.

Stages two (conscious incompetence) and three (conscious competence) on the learning curve are most responsive to the use of performance imagery. The use of performance imagery during stage-one learning could be counterproductive or, at least, less effective since you do not yet know what it is you are supposed to focus on. At this stage of learning however, it would be advantageous to employ psychological imagery to imagine the emotional mind-set one might wish to have in any new activity in which skill level might be low. The idea would be to create a loose, energized, and receptive mind-set that will allow the learning of technique to be as efficient as possible, without the potential problem of frustration at not being able to execute with proficiency yet.

In the fourth stage of learning, psychological imagery regains prominence in the hierarchy of mental skills since excellence in the execution of technique has been developed (and becomes somewhat automatic) over many years of quality practice. What individuals at this stage of skill acquisition often need is to marshal their mental skills to deal with distractions, and to sometimes regain the enthusiasm and desire that fueled their efforts in the early days of their competitive experiences. Passion for the activity or sport in which they are involved on a daily basis does diminish with time even in the most avid competitors, and sometimes these individuals must remind themselves why they are out there week in and week out, accommodating the frustrations and irritations that are part of being successful at the high-performance level. The use of psychological imagery can be helpful in accomplishing this task.

In stage four of the skill-learning process, there is a potential pitfall however that many experienced performers often fall prey to. That pitfall involves complacency. Highly experienced individuals sometimes neglect to control their focus, and they allow their mind to wander to other things—after all, they have "been there and done that" so many times in the past that surely they do not have to work at controlling their focus. Until their lack of correct focus bites them on the butt! In these situations, the use of psychological imagery can be useful to remind the individual to remain sharp and focused, and to pay attention to the important stuff.

CHAPTER 4

Concentration: The Ability to Control Our Focus of Attention

One reason so few of us achieve what we truly want is that we never direct our focus; we never concentrate our power. Most people dabble their way through life, never deciding to master anything in particular.

—TONY ROBBINS, MOTIVATIONAL SPEAKER & AUTHOR

Concentrate all your thoughts upon the work at hand. The sun's rays do not burn until brought to a focus.

—ALEXANDER GRAHAM BELL, SCIENTIST, INVENTOR & ENGINEER

I sometimes got distracted easily and allowed my mind to wander when I needed to be focused. It's quite subtle, really, and just being aware of it helps.

—PAYNE STEWART, PROFESSIONAL GOLFER

Concentration is a fine antidote to anxiety.

—JACK NICKLAUS, PROFESSIONAL GOLFER

"Show me how to focus more effectively, and when I lose my focus, show me how to get it back quickly!"

This is one of the two most common requests I have heard from my clients over the past forty years. And when I conduct group or team seminars and ask the members of the audience what most often stops them from delivering their "A"-game performance at the moment when they are called into action, the issue of distractions (or lack of focus) is raised immediately. This has been a recurring theme that has proven to be universal.

 No matter what culture, language, age, gender, or job function these individuals have come from, they have consistently bemoaned the fact that when they do struggle to perform, preoccupation with other thoughts—what we simply classify as distractions—is at the heart of that struggle.

In fact, many of my clients lead off our discussion with the statement: "sometimes I have a lot of trouble focusing." They are always somewhat surprised when my response is: "I do not believe that this is the real problem you are having and until you get a handle on the real problem, you are not going to be able to fix it as effectively as you might." I then often follow this statement up with this message: "I think that in order for you to have hit the nail on the head precisely, what you should have said is, 'Sometimes, I just cannot seem to control my focus to be on the right thing at the right time. I am focused, but often my focus is directed to the wrong thing, and in those situations, my personal performance suffers'."

No matter what job they do, these individuals invariably recognize that if they are *not focused appropriately* when they are in performance-mode, their performance will not be as good as their true skills suggest that it should.

That is the *real* heart of the problem, is it not? For many people, it is not an issue of being unable to focus (because they actually are focused), but rather, that they are not effective at controlling how they deploy or direct their focus of attention when it is time to perform. They are not effective at directing their thoughts exclusively to the task in front of them.

The ability to focus and control over how we deploy it are not the same thing. In fact, when I evaluate peoples' actual concentration skills in the lab using a variety of computer and other tests over a grueling eight-hour period, many of these same people show me that they have exceptional concentration skills! What is actually going on here? While some individuals truly do have a problem with the ability to sustain their focus for any length of time, what I have observed is that the majority of these individuals actually have phenomenal concentration skills—if they do not sabotage themselves during testing and can figure out how to get out of their own way.

Let us dig into this further to get a clearer understanding of the real problem, and how we might start to address it. As a first step, we will consider what concentration, or focus of attention as it is more accurately described, is and what it is not.

The ability to focus is not a "flat" skill. It is a multidimensional skill that is often not well understood. Consider how often we hear the sharp directive from someone who is not happy with someone else's performance: "You have to focus more!" or "Focus harder!" or yet again, "Darn it! Why don't you just focus?" Is this the solution? Will focusing *more* really solve the problem? Actually, as counterintuitive as it sounds, the truth is that it might very well make the problem worse, if the thing that you are focusing on is the *wrong* thing.

 The correct solution is to ***focus correctly***, based on the situation in front of you.

What most people do not realize is that the ability to mentally focus is a set of skills that can be improved through awareness and quality practice. In order to begin to gain control over your ability to focus, it is important to clearly understand what components make up the skill of concentration and then, how you can manage this "concentration energy" based upon the demands of the situation in that moment.

The skill set we refer to as concentration or focus comprises a series of four different but interrelated components. These are the dimensions of *width* and *direction*, and the qualities of *intensity*, and *duration.*

The *width* component of our focus of attention can vary along a continuum from a *broad* perspective, where a large amount of information coming from a variety of sources must be managed by our internal processor, to a *narrow* one, where only a limited amount of information is allowed to capture our attention in the moment of our performance.

The second dimension of this skill called concentration has to do with the *direction* of our focus. There are occasions when an *internal* focus of attention is necessary (such as when we are pondering the solution to a mental problem, thinking "inside our own head"), and when external events must be selectively filtered, blocked, and set aside. In other instances, however, an *external* focus of attention is more appropriate because we must continue to focus on the changing environment around us in real time, in order to react to it appropriately.

Concentration can also vary in terms of its *intensity*—from being *diffuse* or relatively weak at one end of the continuum to being *intense* at the other.

Finally, concentration can vary in terms of its *duration.* Here, concentration varies from *brief* to *sustained* periods along the time continuum.

We can visually represent the integrated relationship of these various components that make up the skill of concentration as outlined in Figure 9.

You will understand the reasoning behind this statement better when we review the *Rules of the Mental Road*© in the next section of

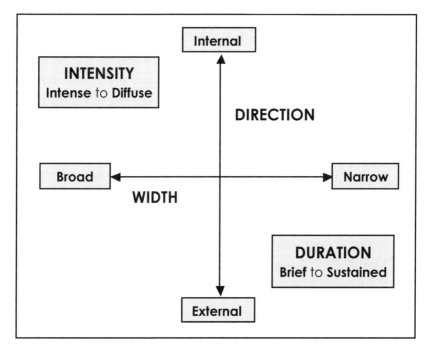

FIGURE 9. The Components of Concentration

this book. Also, there is a direct relationship between the qualities of *intensity* and *duration.* Typically, the more intense your concentration must be, the shorter will be the length of time that you can normally maintain focus at that level of intensity without becoming distracted or mentally fatigued. If on the other hand, only a moderate level of focus is required, you can maintain this state of general, low-level awareness for a much longer period of time without undue mental fatigue.

 It is important that you understand that these components of concentration are *mutually exclusive* in that you cannot concentrate both *broadly* and *narrowly* at the same time, nor can you concentrate both *internally* and *externally* at the same time.

When we remain calm (that is, in the absence of mental anxiety) we are better able to shift amongst these four different components of attention or concentration. In other words, when we are calm, we possess a greater degree of mental flexibility. But under conditions of self-induced pressure (which we often create within ourselves in response to externally imposed "B" factors or our own overriding concern over "results"), we simply allow our emotional stress to build and we subsequently develop negative mind chatter that is associated with fear or worry. In these situations, our focus of attention generally narrows, leading to a deployment of our focus that may not be appropriate for the particular demands of the situation at that time.

The real skill of focus is neither about the ability to focus narrowly or broadly, nor internally or externally in and of itself. It is more about our ability to shift our focus of attention, controlled by us, based on the demands of the situation in which we are engaged. Knowing when and how to shift concentration from one dimension to another based on the demands of the task is a matter of understanding the need to control our focus first, and then of quality practice in exercising this control. This is the holy grail that all high-performance individuals seek to achieve—the ability to control their focus of attention so that it is appropriate to the demands of the task in which they are engaged *in that moment.*

We can use any number of real-world examples to illustrate how a complex and dynamic environment demands that we become proficient in changing the nature of our focus when in execution mode. Let us consider five real-world examples to illustrate the point: a maintenance technician in a manufacturing setting; a golf shot; a surgical intervention in an emergency situation; a security protection detail in a potentially dangerous environment; and landing a fighter jet on an aircraft carrier. (I am sure you would agree these are indeed five very different situations.)

Maintenance Technician

A complex piece of industrial manufacturing equipment requires routine maintenance by skilled technicians to continue to work as intended. In advance of the service call, the technician examines the maintenance log to determine specifically what needs to be accomplished on this call. This requires an external, narrow focus of attention that shifts to become internal as the requirements of the task become clearly understood. As he arrives on-site, the technician ensures that the equipment is powered down and that all of the safety precautions and systems are active and engaged. This initially requires a broad, external focus of attention that becomes narrow and shifts as he considers each system or safety feature in turn. Once he is satisfied that the environment is safe, his focus of attention continues to remain narrow but shifts from external to internal and back again as he reviews the service manual and undertakes the necessary maintenance tasks. He remains fully focused on each task as he is executing it.

It is critical at this stage that his focus be controlled so as not to allow distractions to cause his attention to be diverted to other, nontask-relevant thoughts. If a strong task focus is not maintained throughout the complex maintenance procedures, errors of execution and decision-making may occur and these could subsequently cause major damage to the equipment or operator injury. Once the maintenance has been completed and the checklist has been verified, his focus of attention shifts back to be broad and external as he gives a final check to ensure that no stray tools remain in the work area and that all panels, switches, and breakers have been returned to their correct, post-maintenance position.

Golf Shot

As the golfer approaches his fairway shot, he is scanning his environment (a broad, external focus of attention) to consider where his ball is with respect to where he wants it to go. He may be considering the lie of his ball, any obvious obstacles that might be in his way (trees, bushes, and so forth), from what direction and how hard the wind might be blowing, the position of any hazards in his path (pond, sand trap). As he approaches his ball, his focus shifts internally (still relatively broad in nature) to remember what solutions he has chosen for this kind of situation in the past and calculating how he might adapt a particular solution to this specific situation. As he makes his club selection based on the solution he has decided upon, he addresses his ball and then narrows and lowers his focus of attention to ensure that foot placement, hand position, balance, and so on are good. His focus then shifts up to fix his destination (external, relatively narrow) while reminding himself (internal, relatively narrow) to relax, let his hours of swing practice engage his muscles, and then simply deliver the perfect execution of the shot.

Surgical Intervention

As the surgeon steps into the emergency operating room, she is thinking about the various pieces of information (broad, internal focus) that she has been able to hastily glean from the patient's chart describing his medical history, a summary of the information related to the accident that brought the patient there, an overview of the visible injuries, and medical status as determined by the triage paramedics. As the surgeon approaches the patient, her focus shifts to become external, in order to evaluate the situation first-hand. Moments of shifting from external to internal focus occur on the fly. As the surgeon decides what course of action is demanded by the situation in front of her, she engages the process of the first step. The surgical area is prepped and her focus of attention narrows and intensifies even more as she begins her first cut. As the surgery proceeds, she is constantly managing her focus of attention to be aware of the patient's vital signs, the actions involved in each step of the procedure, and the specific surgical goal that she is attempting to orchestrate.

Security Detail for a Head of State

Security services professionals have a very challenging job. They must remain vigilant at all times (with an external, moderately intense focus) to ensure the safety of the individual(s) whom they are charged to protect. They constantly scan their environment (external, sometimes with a broad, sometimes with a narrow focus) to determine whether there are any developing or immediate threats. They know they cannot sustain an intense focus for hours on end without some degree of "brain fade," so they try to juggle the intensity, based on the situation that they are in. Their job really entails recognizing a threat before it actually becomes one, and the really good ones are very effective at doing so. If and when a threat arises, however, their focus of attention shifts to become external, narrow, and extremely intense as they deal with the threat with an appropriate level of force and/or protect or move their charge to a safer location, or retaliate as necessary.

Landing a Jet on an Aircraft Carrier

As the pilot approaches the ship, she is focused on a broad range of information being supplied to her through her instrumentation and via the radio from the carrier air traffic control center. She is constantly making mental calculations during her descent and physically adjusting her glide path and the plane's attitude based upon the various inputs that she must consider (wind, movement of the boat, and so). The interplay between the processing of new information, its rationalization against information stored in memory from hours of simulation and real-world practice, and the execution of her movements with both hands and feet on the flight controls themselves, represent a dynamic environment that demands flexibility in how the pilot focuses and how she adjusts that focus as the task evolves until she is "wheels on the deck."

While I obviously have not tried to decompose all of the various mental processes engaged in the complex examples above, or pick apart the specific kind of focus employed at each step, I hope that describing the tasks in this simple way will help you to better understand the nature of the dynamic skill of concentration. When you master the ability to shift from broad to narrow focus and back again, and the capacity to maintain the *correct focus* based on the demands of the activity in which you are engaged in that moment, you are better able to avoid irrelevant thoughts since their very existence negatively affects your performance, regardless of what you are doing. Easier said than done, isn't it?

Because controlling focus of attention is so important, I would like to offer a simple, practical imagery technique that you can use to begin to more effectively exert control over how you deploy your focus of attention. I encourage you to think about concentration using the analogy of a flashlight, as illustrated in Figure 10. The flashlight I am referring to is one of those adjustable kinds, where twisting the head adjusts the beam of light to be narrow or wide, depending on the position you select. Think of focus as an adjustable beam of light (like that from a flashlight), where you have full control over the "beam of concentration." You can choose if the focus will be broad, directed to a wide array of objects/information in your environment (such as a floodlight would reveal), or relatively narrow and intense when focused on a specific object or idea (more like a spotlight). This beam of concentration can also be turned inward to consider a broad array of thoughts, images, and feelings, or to a single thought, depending on how narrow your focus is. When your beam of concentration is broad (whether it is directed internally or externally), it takes in a lot of information from a variety of sources, but when it is directed in a narrow way, it intensifies as it is targeted at the object of your focus.

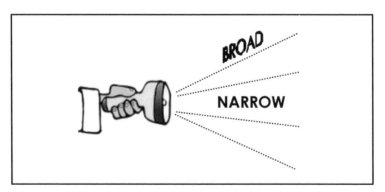

FIGURE 10. Controlling Focus of Attention—Directing Your Beam of Concentration

It should be obvious by now that it is really important to be aware of exactly how your focus is deployed. You must become more proficient at recognizing what the right focus is and become more aware of when your focus is not in the right place. In essence, you must become more effective at *eavesdropping* on your own mind chatter and by doing so, recognizing when your focus of attention is inappropriate. The sooner/earlier you are able to do this, the better off you are from a performance point of view.

Regaining Your Focus

But loss of appropriate focus does occur, even for those high performers who have exceptional concentration skills. What can you do to regain focus when distractions invariably pull you off task?

 Essentially the ability to refocus involves a simple, straightforward, three-step process that must be practiced in order to create an effective skill that can be used on command. The simple process demands that you: *recognize, relax,* and then *refocus.*

Recognize

The first thing you must do is to *recognize* that your focus is inappropriate for the task at hand (that you lost focus, became distracted, and so on). Awareness that you lost focus and how this drift in focus occurred is the first step in correcting the situation. Unless you recognize and acknowledge the loss of focus and ultimately review the factors that led to this loss, you cannot begin to effectively activate the refocusing protocol because you are not even aware that you are losing focus. How many times have you caught yourself in the past with your mind being "somewhere else"? You never even realized that your focus of attention slipped or shifted away from what you were supposed to be focused on to something else, until it hit you squarely in the face! It is also useful to remember that heightened emotions can often get in the way of your ability to recognize what appropriate focus is. Anger, frustration, anxiety, fear, and even exhilaration, for example, can get you thinking about other things and you simply do not realize that your focus is beginning to drift—a process that gradually shifts your thoughts to something that might not be appropriate for your performance in that moment.

Relax

The next step in the refocusing protocol is to *relax*. Actively quiet your mind (turn off the internal mind chatter) and objectively and dispassionately view the fact that your focus of attention is inappropriate for what you are doing *right now*. This action does not take long. It can be accomplished simply by taking a deep breath and purposefully and deliberately choosing to shift your mind-set (your internal flashlight) to reengage an appropriate focus. Once you have practiced this technique enough, just the act of recognizing a loss of appropriate focus is often sufficient to allow you to refocus immediately.

Refocus

Finally, you consciously *refocus*. The act of refocusing your concentration can be facilitated by using self-talk to remind yourself of where your mind is supposed to be. This will often serve to reestablish an appropriate focus of attention. This internal coaching or self-talk is especially beneficial if you explain to yourself what you are trying to accomplish at that very moment—what your immediate action is. It is also important that your self-talk be framed in positive and productive terms; key words like "Relax!", "Be Calm," "Smooth!", "Focus, Here and Now!" can help you to direct your attention and your dominant thought to the actions that are relevant to your performance in that moment. It is a conscious and purposeful repositioning of your mental flashlight.

I would like to close out this chapter dealing with the focus of attention by sharing with you four simple principles or factors that directly affect the quality and nature of our focus. Here are some general rules to keep in mind:

1. We tend to focus on things that are important to us, not on things that aren't.

Wow . . . isn't that surprising! Well, of course it is not really surprising at all, but consider the far-reaching impact of this simple statement. If you are interested in something (whatever it might be), you will focus on it, but if the topic or task in front of you is not of interest to you, you will not generally direct much attention to it.

We see this basic rule played out in schools across the globe every day. Why is it that children sometimes bring home average grades when their parents know that they are smart enough to do better? Our first inclination is to think that they are simply not working hard enough. Another example: how often does a teacher call upon a student to answer a question in class only to have that student seem "spaced out" and not even be aware of what the teacher asked them about? If it happens on a regular basis, the teacher might even begin to suspect that the student suffers from the dreaded affliction that, according to the media, more and more individuals seem to wrestle with—the condition known as attention deficit hyperactivity disorder (ADHD).

But before you give in to this belief, ask yourself this question: When you were in school, did you sometimes allow yourself to become distracted by thoughts that were not related to what you were studying, because the subject matter that was being taught really was of little interest to you? In those situations, where did your mind wander off to (to what thoughts did your internal focus shift to)? I suspect that if you were like me, your thoughts drifted to something that you were actually interested in, something that might have had nothing to do with what was going on at the front of the classroom. Wherever your mind ended up on those extracurricular journeys of the imagination, the net result is that you were simply not paying attention to what the teacher was talking about because you really did not care for the subject. At the time, you believed perhaps that it had zero relevance to your life or you were just bored because the material was too easy.

Students with highly proficient central processing units (the fundamentally brighter kids in the class) often have the hardest time dealing with boredom in these situations. They actually understand what the teacher is trying to get across very early on in the process, but because the instructor must necessarily teach to the bottom end of the class (so that a large number of kids do not get left behind, day in and day out), the sharper kids "check out" mentally as the subject continues to be rehashed in a number of ways. When it comes time to test their knowledge, many of these brighter students achieve decent grades with very little work or study, because they are fundamentally gifted with a fast central processor. Give them material in which they have a genuine interest, however, and they will excel, earning top honors in that subject. They sink their mental teeth into the subject matter because it captivates their interest and their focus of attention, and that directly affects their performance.

It probably would not surprise you that many of my clients report having wrestled with this very issue in their early years, as they were working their way through the school system. This problem plagued them until they got into subject areas that stimulated their interests, or after they left school altogether to engage real life. Then they excelled. Even though the population of individuals that I have been fortunate to work with over the years has generally included highly intelligent people with fundamentally fast central processing units, some of these individuals actually have very little formal schooling. Because some of them did not even graduate from high school, they may not have a great deal of "book learning" behind them, but they are highly intelligent and are capable of analyzing information and making blindingly fast and accurate decisions based on that information. For many of them, this is what keeps them alive.

Now before you are tempted to sit down and write me a letter about my misunderstanding concerning the problem of ADHD, let me make something perfectly clear. I have no doubt that some individuals truly do wrestle with the problem of attention deficit hyperactivety disorder and for these individuals, medication and cognitive training are critical to help them to effectively manage this disorder. Medical/psychological evaluation will of course determine if the condition truly exists, but I believe that this disorder is overly subscribed to. Sometimes it seems to be a catch-all to describe individuals who simply are not very effective at controlling their focus of attention.

Once they understand how they mentally sabotage themselves and how they can avoid these pitfalls, their fundamental ability to focus is actually quite good. When they are engaged in doing something that they enjoy and they learn to adopt the mind-set that optimizes their performance, they do not seem to have much of a problem staying focused (sometimes for hours on end in very demanding situations). They might not be patient enough to sit down and tackle something that does not interest them for more than a few minutes without fidgeting and allowing themselves to become distracted by just about anything, but put them in front of a task that they are interested in and they have absolutely no trouble sustaining their focus of attention appropriately. How many children who are told that they suffer from ADHD can sit in front of a video game console for hours on end without losing focus on the game that they are playing? Does this picture not seem incongruous? If they truly suffer from ADHD, should the disorder not express itself in many of the different things that they do? Or have these individuals simply never learned how to control their focus of attention? Food for thought.

The reality is that we cannot always only do the things that interest us. There are times when we have to deal with material and situations that are not interesting or enjoyable, but the job or task in front of us demands it—like end of the month paperwork or balancing your checkbook. How do we use the first general rule outlined earlier—that we tend to focus better on things that are important to us—to help us to do a more effective job on the things that we are not interested in?

The key is to mentally assign the task some measure of importance and by doing so, ensure that we will automatically tend to focus on it more effectively when it comes time to complete the task. The more we remind ourselves (using self-talk, for example) why the task is important and how it fits in to the repertoire of things that we have to do to accomplish our goals, the more likely we will effectively focus on it when the time comes to get it done. We still may not enjoy it, but we will probably do a better job of completing the task when we do engage it. Not only will we complete the task more quickly with this kind of focus, but we will do a better job overall because our focus will be more appropriate to the demands of what it is that we are doing at that moment.

2. **The more we perceive that a task is new, challenging, and/or complex, the more we will attend to it (that is, focus on it).**

When faced with a new task, the very novelty of that task tends to command our attention automatically. This is also true if we perceive the task in front of us to be challenging and/or complex. On the one hand, the more challenging or difficult a task is, the more we tend to focus on it because we realize that if we do not, we may make mistakes and are not as likely to be successful. We rub our hands together and tell ourselves, "Okay, I'd better get focused here because this isn't going to be easy. Time to buckle down and get my head in the game or I am going to end up being someone's lunch."

On the other hand, if we perceive the task to be very easy, the opposite is true; we probably will not assign it much attention. After all, because we have been there and done that so many times, and we're somewhat expert at this, there really is no need for us to focus all that much. This is when the situation jumps up and bites us hard. When we become complacent, we tend to focus less on what we are doing in that situation, and we allow our mind to wander. This is, in effect, what happens to us when we get bored, where the task that we are engaged in no longer captivates our attention and our mind starts to drift to other things.

Indeed, this simple rule explains why experienced performers sometime make rookie mistakes. They perceive the task in front of them to be simple, and they believe that they have it covered, without the need for them to give what they are doing much thought.

Even if the job is inherently dangerous, their substantial familiarity and experience with the procedures and process can lull them into a sense of complacency where they believe they simply do not have to think about it much, until something bad happens.

When I was younger, one of my childhood friends started to work for a manufacturing company after he graduated from high school. His job was physical, but relatively straightforward and easy. He operated a large stamping machine where raw sheets of flat metal entered the machine from one side, and where he then positioned the piece and activated the press with his foot to "stamp" out a floor pan when it was in place. After a year or so of doing this work, one day he just was not paying attention to what he was doing. After all, he had done this simple task tens of thousands of times before. He was thinking about something else, and yet he pushed the button and the press came down. He left half of his hand in the machine. If you think this is an isolated example, the next time you find yourself at a convention of master cabinetmakers or wood workers, check out their hands. You might be surprised to find that many of them are missing at least part of a digit.

Interestingly, the research in this area tells us that at the other end of the difficulty continuum, the same is also true. If we perceive that the task in front of us is too difficult and most certainly beyond our abilities, our focus of attention to that task also diminishes. It appears that our focus is held most effectively when we perceive the task in front of us to be challenging but doable. If we believe that there is no way we can be successful completing the task, our focus of attention on that task deteriorates as we mentally "give up." It ties back somewhat to the issue of confidence. We must believe that we can be successful if we are to more effectively sustain our focus of attention on the actions that can lead to success. This basic principle becomes important when assigning complex tasks to employees. To ensure the greatest chance of success, match the skill sets and knowledge of the doer to the task being done.

3. **Our focus of attention easily and naturally shifts toward things that are unexpected, whereas things that are constant become somewhat invisible over time.**

The more the situation in which we find ourselves remains the same or is unchanging, the more likely we are to lose focus in that environment. That which is going on around us dissolves into the background and effectively disappears, until something changes and this new stimulus snags our attention. A couple of simple examples to illustrate the point:

- If you have ever lived beside a busy highway, you will remember that when you first moved there, you could not get a decent night's sleep for the first week or so because of vehicle noise. Especially the big trucks! Relatively quickly, however, you got to the point where you did not even hear the noise coming from the many vehicles on the road, and you were able to sleep without any problems whatsoever, regardless of the volume of traffic. And yet, in that same environment, you wake up instantly when someone in the house drops a glass on the floor.

- When you first take off in a plane, for the first ten minutes or so, the cabin environment seems really loud and you cannot even imagine how you will be able to sleep or even rest. Within a few minutes though, the engine and wind noise falls into the background, and you are no longer even conscious of the noise in the environment, until the pitch on one of the engines changes and your focus of attention is drawn to it immediately.

When we discussed the selective filtering process in Chapter 2, we considered how humans process information at the most fundamental level. I mentioned that the basic purpose of this selective filtering process is to protect us from being overloaded by so much sensory information that our central processor is not able to function. One of the natural by-products of this selective filtering and adaptation process is what is known as "acclimation." Our central nervous system has developed the capacity over the millennia to tune out sensory information that is unchanging and, therefore, on the evolutionary scale, not particularly relevant for us to focus on. If we were not able to tune out all of this external stimulation in a systematic (and automatic) way, our brain would be overtaxed and we could never get any rest. Because we are limited in how much information we can process at any one time, we have evolved such that the constant stuff gets suppressed over time, whereas the unexpected or new stuff is what tends to command our attention.

This shift is known as an *orienting reflex*. Unexpected or changing things—because they are indeed unexpected and changing—cause us to *orient* or direct our focus of attention to them. This is a central nervous system reflex that we do not even have to think about because it happens automatically, mediated by our unconscious mind. This is a very good thing. Consider how useful it is that on a busy, bustling street where there is all kinds of noise, a car horn or a shout immediately causes us to shift our focus of attention to the oncoming car that is about to run us over. This orienting reflex also can be problematic, though, when our natural tendency to shift our focus toward unexpected and perhaps unimportant things distracts us from the very thing that we should remain focused on.

4. **Visual distractions in our environment are generally more powerful than those from other sensory modalities.**

It is estimated that in a normally sighted individual, 80 percent or more of the information that gets through to our central processor passes via the visual channel. As a result, the sense of vision is the most powerful conduit of information for a normally sighted individual, and perhaps this is why the skill of *imagery* is so influential and pervasive in the human species. In fact, engineers rely on this rule when they design a lot of our equipment today. In automobiles, airplanes, and indeed most complex pieces of equipment, we use warning lights or gauges, sometimes with the added "bump" of sound, to alert the operator to a problem. As soon as that flashing light blinks on, even if it is only perceived in our peripheral vision, our focus of attention shifts immediately and is redirected to the light and to take note of the problem. How many people do you know whose focus of attention shifts immediately when the blinking light on their Blackberry or smart phone signals the arrival of a text message or an e-mail?

I suspect that you have probably experienced this response yourself. When you are driving along in your automobile with your eyes fixed on the road ahead, what happens to your focus of attention when the little red light in the dash—the one shaped like a small tap or oil can—comes on? Even though you only pick up the light in your peripheral vision when it comes on, your focus of attention immediately shifts from the road to the light. Again, it is a different representation of the orienting reflex discussed above. Think about how many times you have been distracted by things in your visual environment, and even though you are trying to stay focused on something, your focus of attention naturally (and sometimes way too easily) shifts to that distracting object or item in your visual environment: the good looking person walking by, the flashy car, an important person who may have just walked into the room, and so on.

 The long and the short of it is this: the main challenge that we all face when we engage our moments of performance is not to "pay attention," but rather, *what to pay attention to*!

PART TWO

A Simple Framework for Performance *Thinking:* The Seven Key *Rules of the Mental Road*©

Introduction

Even though my vocation provides me with the opportunity to work one-on-one with high performers in the real world, I view my role simply as that of an educator. Ultimately, if I can teach my clients how to bait their hook and cast their line with precision, they will learn how to fish successfully on their own. While I try to play a supporting role as they work to implement this way of thinking into their life and their work—especially in the early stages of the skill acquisition process—once they understand the basic principles regarding how humans mentally process information, and how this processing either supports our ability to perform or sabotages it, they are well on their way to understanding how to optimize their own performance. Then, with a simple but powerful tool like the A.C.T. Model© process, they can begin to systematically take control of and reprogram their way of thinking, and realize all the benefits that this Performance *Thinking* brings about.

Many years ago, I created the *Rules of the Mental Road*© as a basic framework that could serve as the backbone upon which to build this educational process. While the rules are simple—and I suspect that some people might even consider them to be "simplistic"— they are powerful because they speak to how the way that we mentally process information directly influences the quality of our personal performance. I formulated these rules based upon my personal observations over the years and on background information such as that which we discussed in the first section of this book: the performance equation ("A" x "B" = Results); how our mind processes information; how imagery impacts performance; and how the skill of concentration actually works. Over the decades, these rules have proven to be:

- *Fundamental,* in that they are simple and underlie the thought processes that either allow us to perform to the best of our ability or sabotage us as we engage in the performance itself.

- *Universal,* because they apply to everyone. It does not matter what culture people come from, what language they speak, how old they are, what their gender is, or what their activity or interest might be. These simple rules have directly applied to every one of my clients. They all have recognized the validity of these simple rules in their life and work.

- *Infallible,* since they have yet to be proven incorrect.

Respecting the rules will allow you to shape your thinking so that you will be able to perform to the best of your ability when called upon to do so. Adopting a mind-set that violates the rules will most definitely affect your personal performance in a negative way. As a consequence, the results that you achieve will not be the best that you are capable of in that situation or performance. If you make the choice to embrace the mind-set of Performance *Thinking,* you will be better able to develop the kind of mental control that will lead to that sought-after but elusive quality high performance individuals often refer to as mental toughness. Fortunately, we do not have to understand all the intricacies of how the mind works to accomplish this goal. We just need to keep a few simple rules in mind.

CHAPTER 5

RULE #1

If You Want to Climb Out of a Hole, the Very First Thing You Must Do Is Stop Digging!

The best thinking has been done in solitude. The worst has been done in turmoil.
—THOMAS A. EDISON, INVENTOR

I never looked at the consequences of missing a big shot . . . when you think about the consequences you always think of a negative result.
—MICHAEL JORDAN, NBA HALL OF FAME INDUCTEE & BUSINESSMAN

Once you replace negative thoughts with positive ones, you'll start having positive results.
—WILLIE NELSON, COUNTRY MUSIC SINGER-SONGWRITER

Have you ever found yourself in a mental funk and were not really sure exactly how you got there? When you ultimately became conscious of just how bad a place you were in mentally, you wondered how your thoughts shifted to become so negative. The *decay* in your thinking was gradual and insidious, and you were not even aware that it was happening until you "woke up" somewhere down in that deep, maybe even dark, emotional hole. And the simple truth is, the deeper the mental hole we are in, the harder it is and the longer it takes to climb out of it!

Think about this rule for a moment and consider it literally. If you were indeed in a real hole that was ten-feet deep, charged with the act of digging, it would be impossible for you to continue digging and climb out of that hole at the same time. You would not be able to accomplish both actions simultaneously because they are mutually exclusive. If your eyes are fixed to the ground beneath your feet, and you are flailing away with the shovel, it would not be possible to climb out of that hole at the same time. This basic rule holds true when we consider how the human mind works.

If you want to think positively and productively, the very first thing you must do is stop thinking negatively and destructively. This is simply because our central processor cannot be processing a good thought and a bad thought at the same moment in time. Sometimes we dig ourselves into a mental hole by incessantly dwelling on negative thoughts that tend to become dominant, pervasive, and overriding. This negative thinking corrupts the mindset that optimizes our ability to do our best work. These negative thoughts gain strength and power the more we process them, and before we know it, we are staring at the bottom of a hole while continuing to dig furiously. We end up so far down that hole of negative thinking that we cannot seem to find the way out. What does this act of mental digging look like?

By and large, the act of mental digging takes the form of *worry:* a negative film loop and its associated negative mind chatter that we constantly replay in our mind, dwelling on all the negative possibilities that might occur even before they have. We worry about whether we will be good enough, whether we will be able to achieve the results we so desperately want, and what others might think of us if we fail. This self-doubt cripples us and corrupts our performance because our focus shifts to the things that we are worried about, rather than to what we should be focused on in that moment. How often do you catch yourself dwelling with regret on the perceived negative consequences of your own past mistakes? Does this internal self-recrimination influence your performance when you find yourself in such a moment of turmoil?

Reflect back to the four groups of high performers we considered when we discussed the *performance equation* in the first section of this book (see page 34). How much of their focus of attention was deployed to the act of execution itself (the "A" in the equation—the only thing that they can control) as opposed to the potential problems that might lead to failure (the "B" factors) or to the "Results" themselves. If you recall, only approximately 58 percent of their central processor was focused on the act of execution (while they were engaged in the act of executing) as opposed to approximately 42 percent of their central processor being directed to things that were outside of their direct control. Even the best in the world do it when they are not on top of their game. Who of us has not entertained this kind of thinking, perhaps more than we would like to acknowledge?

FIGURE 11. The Act of Mental Digging

"Show me how to keep my confidence high,
especially when things are not going well."

The more we worry about failing and the more we focus on the outcome, the harder it is for us to deliver the quality of execution, in the moment, that ultimately yields the result we are seeking. The more we doubt ourselves and focus on things that we cannot control, the greater is our level of anxiety in that moment because our thoughts are directed not to our actions but to the consequences of our actions.

 We shift out of the mode of doing and slip into judgment mode, processing how well or how poorly we think we are doing as we are doing it.

The real problem here is that by allowing ourselves to think negatively, we become incapable of thinking positively at the same time, and our performance suffers. This act of digging is the basis for the loss of confidence that has become such a way of life for many people as they contemplate the many challenges that they must face.

Rule #1 affirms that you must first put the shovel down if you are going to be successful in shifting your mind-set to positive and productive thinking. To accomplish this important first step, you must first become *aware* that you are thinking incorrectly (negatively) and then *choose* to process positive and productive thoughts. If you do not consciously and willfully stop the digging and put the shovel down, you will not be able to deliberately shift your dominant thought to the kind of positive and productive thinking you need to turn yourself around and climb out of the mental hole you have dug for yourself.

Is the secret then the power of positive thinking? Well, yes and no. Yes, in that it is far better to possess a positive mind-set than a negative one, and we will expand on this statement as we review Rule #3 of the Mental Road© a little later in this section. But no, in that it is not good enough in a demanding performance environment to only be positive. Your thought processes must also be productive, and by productive I specifically mean task-focused. I have met many people who are very positive individuals but who do not perform particularly well because even though they are positive, they do not effectively control their focus of attention to be in the moment, fully present and connected to the act of performing. They are positive, happy people who see life's glass as being half-full, but are often scattered or unfocused in their thinking. They do not seem to control their focus very effectively. How do we respect Rule #1 in the way that we think?

 The first step is to become vigilant for negative thinking, to *eavesdrop* on our own internal mind chatter and catch ourselves as we begin to think negatively or counterproductively. It is the art of self-listening that involves paying attention to (being aware of) the little creature that sits on our shoulder and whispers in our ear . . . and ultimately controlling what he/she says!

How often do we allow that little creature to whisper suggestions and thoughts that undermine our ability to perform, rather than support it? The sooner we become aware of the tone of the feedback we give ourselves and control it to be both positive and productive, the sooner we will stop digging, put the shovel down, and begin to climb out of the hole. This is also where mentors, coaches, or advisors can be particularly helpful as they can point out to you when your attitude is in need of adjustment. When we are caught in the middle of a downward spiraling thought process, we are not always conscious that we are slipping into that dark hole. Sometimes it just takes a comment from a trusted friend to point out the obvious to us.

The good news is that we create our own set of mental images and thoughts in our conscious mind that directly influence—through the action of our unconscious mind—our feelings, the behaviors that flow from those emotions, and our ability to perform.

The bad news is that we create our own set of mental images and thoughts in our conscious mind which in turn—through the actions of our unconscious mind—directly influence our feelings, the behaviors that flow from those emotions, and our ability to perform.

The first *Rule of the Mental Road*© demands that we be vigilant for the wrong kind of thinking and squash it as soon as we recognize it. We then must replace it with the right kind of thinking.

CHAPTER 6

RULE #2
The Mind Can Only Actively Process One Thought at a Time

A man who can drive safely while kissing a pretty girl
is simply not giving the kiss the attention it deserves.

—ALBERT EINSTEIN, THEORETICAL PHYSICIST & AUTHOR

The focus and the concentration and the attention to detail
that flying takes is a kind of meditation. I find it restful
and engaging, and other things slip away."

—HARRISON FORD, ACTOR & PILOT

When you write down your ideas you automatically focus your
full attention on them. Few if any of us can write one thought
and think another at the same time. Thus a pencil and
paper make excellent concentration tools.

—MICHAEL LEBOEUF, AUTHOR & MANAGEMENT PROFESSOR

Let me share an exercise with you that illustrates how the mind can only focus actively on one thing at a time. Because this test will not work as well in this format with me trying to guide you, the reader, I would like you to try this exercise with someone else. I will explain to you what I would like you to do, and you can guide them through it. Tell them—it could be a single person or a group

117

of people, it does not matter—that it is a simple, mental processing task that you would like their help to investigate. It is important that they focus on the task, so get them to relax and simply pay attention to what you are going to ask them to do.

Explain to the individual or group that this simple mental task consists of counting backwards from 100 by 3s, out loud, but only when you ask them to begin. Tell them that while they are accomplishing this task, you are going to also give them a simple mathematical problem that you want them to solve and call out the answer to, once they have solved it. Tell them to begin counting backwards, and when they get to 91, say "$2 \times 3 = \_\_$". Observe what happens.

You can probably guess even before you conduct this little experiment what is going to happen, but I will share with you here what *always* happens when I do this with my clients, whether one-on-one or with groups in seminars.

Some people are obviously better with numbers than others. Some individuals are able to count backwards from 100 by 3s much more quickly and with less difficulty than others, but regardless of the cognitive strategy that they utilize to accomplish the task, when they engage the process you can see that they are internally focused on the specific challenge you have given them. They call out the sequence of numbers in the correct order for the most part. Then, when you ask them to solve the simple equation "$2 \times 3 = \_\_$", what happens? They first recognize that you asked them a question. They then stop processing the task of counting backwards, and their internal focus of attention shifts as they dip into auditory memory to understand the question that you gave them. They consider the math problem you asked them to solve, they quickly calculate the answer and give it—"6"—and then their internal focus of attention subsequently shifts back to the original task. Before they re-engage the original task, however, they must again dip into short-term memory to determine where they were in their counting sequence and then re-engage the process with the same cognitive strategy that they employed at the outset. We can describe the process of what took place from a cognitive point of view with the simple flow diagram shown in Figure 12.

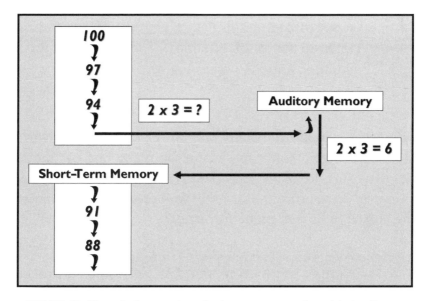

FIGURE 12. The mind can only actively process one thought at a time.

The truth is, if we could actively process two thoughts at the same time, we should be able to continue the task of counting backwards by 3s *without interruption,* while at the same time calculating our answer to the simple mathematical problem. Would it surprise you to find out that no one can effectively do both at the same time? So why does this happen and what is actually going on here?

The human brain is capable of millions of computations each second but our mind can only *consciously* process this information one piece at a time. (Remember the reference librarian we discussed in Chapter 2?). For all intents and purposes, the mind is not capable of processing two thoughts at the same time! Many people believe that they can actively process more than one thought at a time, but in practical terms they cannot—they misunderstand what multitasking is.

What happens when we multitask is that we switch back and forth between different thoughts, albeit very quickly indeed sometimes (in thousandths of a second), but still it is a process of shifting our internal focus of attention from one thought to another, and then back again.

If we try to juggle too many balls at the same time, however—that is to say, we attempt to engage too many tasks at the same time—we start to make mistakes. This often leads to failure because we do not focus sufficiently well on any of them. So, what is the impact of Rule #2 on performance?

Simply put, if your mind is only able to process one thought at a time, you had better make certain that it is directed to the right thought, one that is relevant to your performance in that moment.

The implications of this rule are significant. If you are focused on this (whatever "this" might be), you cannot be processing that (whatever "that" might be) at that same moment in time. Stated another way, if you are focused on the right thing, you cannot actively be processing the wrong thing at the same time. If, on the other hand, you are focused on the wrong thing, you cannot be actively processing the right thing at the same time.

This is why, when we talked about concentration and focus in Chapter 4, I said that it is not our inability to focus our attention on a task that is the problem, but our lack of control over how we *deploy* our focus of attention in the moment when we must perform. It is a question of where we direct our beam of concentration.

If you think back to the performances in your life that you would categorize as being amongst your best ever, it is likely that you would report having a single-minded focus directed specifically to the task in which you were involved, where your mind was fully absorbed in the process of what you were doing. This process-focused, undistracted, here-and-now mind-set is a common theme reported by most of my clients at the moment of their most brilliant performances, whether it is in the arts, in sport, in business, or whatever. Some people refer to it as being "in the zone." Assuming then that you can indeed only actively process one thought at a time (Rule #2), what would the consequence be if your focus was directed to something other than what is required at that very moment? For example:

- Worrying about how you are being perceived by others or perhaps fearing that you are not performing well enough to achieve your goal or live up to someone's expectations.

- Worrying about whether the results will be good enough rather than being focused fully on the process of execution—that is, thinking about winning the game, winning the championship; making your monthly sales quota, and so on, instead of focusing on the actions that will lead you to this goal, while you are engaged in the act of execution itself.

- In general terms, being distracted by unrelated thoughts that are not directly beneficial or relevant to your performance at that very moment; and so on.

The consequence of having your mind occupied with processing thoughts that are not related to your performance is that it makes it impossible to be focused fully on the process of performing at the same time, in the moment. It is likely that your performance in whatever you are doing will not be as good as it could otherwise be. It does not automatically mean that you will necessarily be unsuccessful; it just means that your personal performance will not be optimized and your part in the performance will not be as good as it could have been. It might lead to failure as it often does, but then again it may not.

 It is important that you realize that it does not matter whether it is a good thought or a bad thought, if it is the wrong thought because it is not relevant to your performance in that moment, your performance will likely suffer.

You would be surprised how many very successful high-performance athletes and occupational professionals have acknowledged to me instances where they were very near to a significant success only to see that success evaporate in an instant because they made an error in thinking. They allowed their thoughts to shift as they approached their goal and started to focus on victory, on the Olympic podium, or on counting their money for the win, but the event was not over yet! Their focus of attention shifted from execution—which is what up to that point put them in a position to win—to seeing that win evaporate because their focus shifted to *thoughts* of winning and images associated with the celebration of that event. For example, a racer's focus was incorrect as he drove into the last corner (because his mind was already in Victory Lane), and he simply threw the car off the track. Remember the basic truth of the "A" x "B" = Results equation!

One of the most common problems that I have observed over the years that arises in all walks of life because of the very existence of Rule #2, is that people often become overwhelmed and suffer increased mental anxiety when they feel like their mind is being "swamped" by too many things to do or too much information that they must somehow wrap their head around. It has proven to be a fundamental problem that almost all of us wrestle with at one time or another. How often do you feel overloaded when you have so much on your plate that you must deal with, and when you do wrestle with this issue, you end up emotionally and mentally drained, confused, and unable to think straight? It is a problem that is infinitely more common than you might think, and it occurs fundamentally because of Rule #2.

Often we are placed, or we place ourselves, in situations where the challenge we must deal with requires us to take in a lot of information (say from our external environment, where people or circumstances are pulling us in different directions, all seemingly at the same time) and put that information into our central processor where we can effectively deal with it. We feel as though we are being torn apart because we have so much information to process, and we become overwhelmed mentally and somewhat discombobulated. We just cannot seem to keep things straight in our mind because of all the competing thoughts and information that we are trying to consider. Why does this happen and what can we do about it?

Let us use a simplistic analogy to dissect the problem and understand what basic strategies we might use to mitigate the negative effects of trying to deal with too much information on our performance. The analogy we will use is that of a reservoir and a funnel, and the problem can be illustrated with a simple diagram (see Figure 13) where the oval in the diagram represents our mind (the reservoir of our conscious thoughts, memories, and so forth). The exterior part of the diagram, outside the oval, represents our environment—the thing that we must typically interact with as we gather information and then execute actions as we perform. The funnel is in place to describe how we process information from a mental point of view. We must often take in a lot of information from our external environment as we receive cues from the things going on around us, and somehow get it into our mind so that we can process it. But the shape of the funnel is defined by Rule #2. While we can import a lot of information through our senses, we can only actively process it into our mind one thought at a time. The skinny end of the funnel exists because of the bottlenecked "reference librarian" we talked about in Chapter 2.

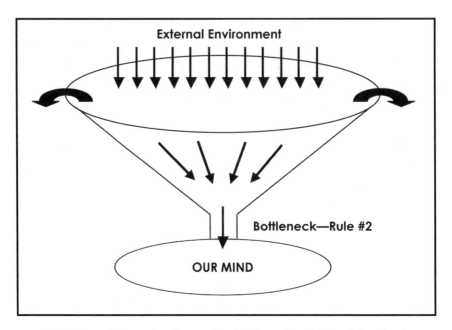

FIGURE 13. Information Processing Bottleneck and Mental Overload

Let us now consider our analogy more literally. Assume we had twelve gallons of milk and that we popped the tops off all of them and poured them into the funnel at the same time. Assuming that the output pipe of our funnel is the same size as the opening of one gallon of milk, and that the size of the funnel itself is equal to the volume of two of those gallons of milk, what are the consequences that will arise from this action? Clearly, if we try to pour all twelve gallons into the funnel at the same time—because we are trying to get all of the milk into our reservoir at the same time—there will be an overflow that will occur as milk spills over the side and onto the floor. We have essentially asked the funnel to process more fluid per unit of time than it can because of the bottleneck that limits the amount that actually can pass into the reservoir. Likewise, when we try to process too much information (from a variety of sources perhaps) *at the same time,* we get spillage (overload), and a mess (feeling overwhelmed) occurs because fundamentally, we can only process the information one thought at a time.

The significant challenge we face in this situation is to get all this information into our mind without becoming overloaded and losing the ability to keep our dominant thoughts sorted and task-relevant. Once we are able to get the information into our mind, the selective deployment of our focus of attention and the choice of dominant thought that we apply in the moment will determine how effectively we take action and perform. How can we mitigate this natural tendency to become somewhat overwhelmed when faced with a lot of information that we must process? There are two simple strategies that can help.

1. The first strategy involves being well organized. If we use our milk jug analogy, when we organize the arrival of the jugs into three waves of four gallons each rather than a single wave of twelve gallons all at the same time, we reduce the amount of spillage or overload that occurs (Figure 14). By being better organized, we can more effectively regulate the amount of information we must process at any given time and reduce the

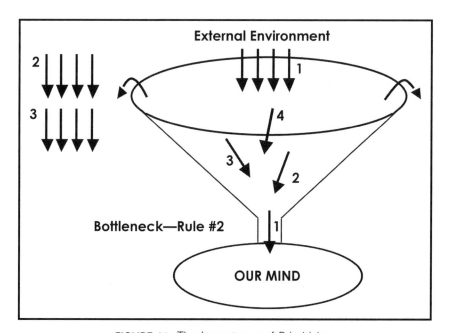

FIGURE 14. The Importance of Prioritizing

tendency to feel overwhelmed by the need to consider so much information in such a narrow window of time. If we manage our time effectively, we do not end up leaving so much to be dealt with at the last minute.

The truth is that even when we are well organized, we may still end up with a lot of stuff that must be dealt with at the last minute. While it will not be as bad as it might have been, there may still be some overload if we attempt to process those four gallons all at the same time. After all, our funnel maxes out with the volume of two gallons.

2. The second strategy involves the act of sorting our choices to prioritize the tasks that we must still process—that is, to continue the milk jug metaphor, sorting our four jugs of milk in order of priority and then ruthlessly focusing on pouring each through the funnel, one jug at a time.

It does not mean that we only attend to a single task until it is completed, but rather we multitask in a way that allows us to focus on each task in turn, fully connected to it when we are engaged in that task until the point where it is appropriate to set it aside in favor of shifting our focus (willfully and purposefully) to another task, when it is appropriate to do so.

The problem for many people is that they do not exercise this kind of control over their focus of attention but allow the environmental situation around them to define their focus of attention. And since there is a lot going on in their environment, their head seems to be on a swivel where their focus of attention is dragged back and forth, up and down, at such a rate and in so many directions that they become cross-eyed and cannot think straight.

Rule #2 simply states that the mind can only actively process one thought at a time, and this rule demands that our focus of attention be directed to the correct thing at the correct time—the holy grail of the performance equation.

CHAPTER 7

RULE #3

You Can't *NOT* Think about Whatever Is on Your Mind

Instead of focusing on the circumstances that you cannot change—focus strongly and powerfully on the circumstances that you can.

—JOY PAGE, ACTRESS

The competition is one aspect of the job, but I think if you're too busy worrying about the competition, you don't focus enough on what you're doing.

—KATIE COURIC, JOURNALIST

Question: The more you try *not* to think about something, what typically happens? *Answer:* The more you tend to think about it.

The human mind cannot act positively in direct response to a negative thought. By expressing things in the negative, whether you state them out loud or simply process them as internal mind chatter, you are in fact directing your thoughts to be focused on exactly what you did not want to do, picturing the performance or its outcome in your mind's eye exactly the way you did not want to do it.

> Because your unconscious mind takes its direction from your conscious, dominant thoughts, the more you try *not* to think about something, the more the image or outcome which you are trying to avoid gains strength and shape, as it is conjured up with your mind's eye.

It does not matter whether the thought you are considering is a positive one or a negative one, whatever thought you are processing becomes dominant, and it directs your unconscious mind to lead you to feel, behave, and perform in a certain way.

Here is a simple exercise to help drive the point home. Again, because it will likely not be as effective if I direct this exercise to you, the reader, I ask that you try it with someone who is close at hand. Read through the instructions first and then come back and try it out. The simple process of this exercise is to ask the participant first to relax and then give them the following instruction:

"I DO NOT want you to think about the thing that I am going to describe for you now. I do NOT want you to picture in your mind's eye . . .

A HUGE PINK ELEPHANT . . . pause

Wearing . . . PURPLE BOXER SHORTS . . . pause

With . . . BIG YELLOW DOTS all over them . . ."

Pause again for a moment. Ask them how they did and whether they ended up picturing the pink elephant with purple shorts covered in big yellow dots. It is difficult to avoid "seeing" it in our mind's eye, is it not? Even though we understand the instruction not to think about the elephant, in most instances we are not able to prevent ourselves from creating that very picture in our mind. Remember, the human mind essentially thinks in pictures.

If we wanted to avoid seeing the image of the pink elephant in our mind's eye, we would need to rely on and utilize the principle behind Rule #2. We would direct our conscious, dominant thought to process something else, another image that grabs our attention fully (for example, that of a big orange squirrel with a long, red, bushy tail). The vast majority of people who try this little exercise end up picturing that strange pink elephant in all of its glory, even when they fully understood the explicit instruction you gave them not to do so. What is the impact of Rule #3 on your personal performance? Quite simply, you can't *not* think about whatever is on your mind, and whatever that thought is, your unconscious mind seeks to make it happen.

In order to examine this statement from a different perspective, I would like you to consider the following two scenarios involving a driving coach giving instructions to a young, aspiring race car driver:

Scenario One: "Now, whatever you do, John, don't get out too wide going into corner three. There is a lot of dust and rubber on the outside portion of the track in corner three, and if you get your right front tire out there, the front end is going to wash out and the car will push right off the track in the middle of the corner. If that happens, you will end up planting the nose of your car straight into the tire barriers, right near the big yellow bush. So whatever you do, don't let the car swing out too wide going into corner three!"

Now that you have read this script, sit back for a moment and examine the imagery that was generated as you read these words. Did you picture the car getting wide going into corner three, getting out onto the slippery part of the track, and then sliding off the track into the tire barriers? I suspect that for the vast majority of readers, this is exactly what you pictured in your mind's eye. Now contrast this to the following script:

Scenario Two: "Okay, John, when you head into corner three, don't let the car swing out too wide because there is dust on the outside of the track and it could be treacherous. What I want you to do when you roll into corner three is keep the nose of the car pinned down to the inside portion of the track. Put the left front tire down against the white line on the very inside of the track and let it roll along the edge of that white line. When you see the big oak tree in front of you, let out some steering input so that you head directly for it. That will give you the right line heading toward corner four."

Again, take a moment to consider the imagery associated with this script. Quite different, is it not? Which script do you believe will help the young driver optimize his or her performance and which one will help them to actually sabotage themselves?

 So often, we mentally pre-program ourselves (and others) for failure by openly expressing things negatively and just as importantly, thinking about them in the negative, not realizing what kind of impact those instructions might yield.

Consider the following statements:

- "Don't get nervous. There is nothing to be nervous about," just before you take the stage for the big recital.

- "Don't mess up this time. If you mess up again, we will be in big trouble," just before you take the field for the big game.

- "This is a really important account for the company. Don't screw it up or you will be in real trouble!", driving anxiety through the roof just before you step into the room to negotiate the big contract.

- "You can give it a try if you want to, but no one is buying. You are probably wasting your time," creating an expectation of rejection and failure;

- "Whatever you do, don't crash the car! We don't have enough spare parts to get it fixed."

- "When you are up on stage, Billy, don't focus on the crowd."

- "Make sure you don't slice the ball into the rough on the right side of the fairway. It's treacherous there and you will never be able to get out of there cleanly."

- "How many times have I told you *not* to . . ."

As the statements above serve to illustrate, we frequently have a tendency to express comments in a manner that incites others as well as ourselves, via that little voice that speaks to us in our head, to perform more poorly. We do not even realize the consequences of our statements. In these examples, the predominant image we *implant* into the mind of the receiver at the moment of their performance is the very action that we hope they will avoid! We offer the directive "don't be nervous, angry, or frustrated," but the very picture we implant in their mind is that of them being nervous, angry, or frustrated! Visions of the big, pink elephant.

As the dominant mental program at that moment, the mental blueprint for their performance, the images of incorrect execution or behavior that they picture in their mind are translated into a sequence of physical actions that result in more easily achieving that very outcome. Remember the principles related to the topic of imagery we discussed in Chapter 3. In such situations, it is almost impossible not to suffer a breakdown in performance, unless the individual can learn to replace the faulty program with a positive, productive, or task-focused one.

If you are to optimize your own performance, or that of others you might be coaching or mentoring, it is critical that you frame the discussion and your instructions so as to clearly outline what the correct execution entails. This does not mean that we never express what we do not want them to do, because they need to know what the wrong thing looks like too. It is just that we do not leave it there. We follow the brief cautionary note with an expanded expression of what the right performance looks like, feels like, smells like, and tastes like when it is executed with perfection. If we are successful in implanting this dominant thought into their mind, their unconscious mind is more likely to take them to that place. Their performance will likely be closer to the best that they are capable of and, other than the influence of potential "B" factors, the results they achieve will be as good as they are capable of in that situation. Of course, the same applies to us.

The sad truth unfortunately is that we sabotage ourselves routinely by violating this simple rule.

 Our overriding thought as we step into the performance often is directed toward the very things we hope will not occur: crashing; becoming anxious and tongue-tied; stumbling over our words and thoughts; failing and what the consequences of that failure might represent; what others might think of us if we do fail, and so on.

Rule #3 simply affirms that the harder you try *not* to think about something, the more strength that negative thought and its associated negative images gain and become firmly entrenched in your mind. You must learn to phrase things (and picture them) in your mind in positive terms, describing to yourself how you want to think and feel while you successfully accomplish the task that you are focused on, rather than what you do not want to do. This is why it is better to have a positive thought than a negative one, but also why that thought should be performance-relevant, rather than just positive. Consider for a moment how sabotaging our instructions can be when the only thing we offer is feedback regarding what someone may have done incorrectly, or give directives in advance of a major performance where we constantly tell ourselves or the individual involved what we do not want them to do.

Since you can't *not* think about what is on your mind, and because you can actively process only one thought at a time, you must ensure that the thoughts you choose to process in your mind are associated with the act of performing, picturing in your mind's eye what you want to do, how you want to do it, and how it feels when you do it exactly that way.

As a final thought in this chapter, I would like to address the issue of sleep, or more correctly, the inability some people have to get restful sleep. Over the years, many of my clients and people I have spoken with have expressed having difficulty sleeping because they cannot quiet their mind. This is often associated with periods when they must deal with difficult challenges or just before an important competition where there is a lot at stake. Their mind races in the still of the night and they simply cannot fall sleep. You can look to Rule #3 to explain why this happens and how we can stop it from doing so. The solution is simple enough, although it is not easy to implement initially.

Remember, you can't *not* think about whatever is on your mind. In advance of the big event or competition, if you are worrying about whether you will be successful, whether it will come to pass as you hope it will, or whether you will achieve your goal or not, your anxiety increases as you become preoccupied with these thoughts. Even though you recognize at the conscious level that these things are outside of your control, you continue to process these concerns. Your mind is a whirlwind of jumbled thoughts. If you keep telling yourself to not think about these things as you lay there tossing and turning, what happens? The more you get frustrated because you cannot sleep, the more you tend to dig a mental hole. So long as you are digging a hole and beating yourself up because you cannot stop thinking about things that you do not want to think about, the more you think about them. That preoccupation prevents your mind from quieting.

How can you use Rule #3 to help solve this common problem? As simple as it sounds, you have to control your conscious thoughts and direct them to images and thoughts that are benign and relaxing. This is the fundamental premise of the relaxation techniques used in yoga and other forms of meditation. By focusing on the slow rhythm of your own breathing as you inhale and exhale, and the associated relaxing of your muscles, your mind is drawn away from the thoughts that are occupying your mind and perhaps are causing you stress. This is also where the strategy of counting sheep comes into play. If you direct your thoughts to something that has no emotional baggage or consequence (such as the counting of imaginary sheep jumping over your bed; the soft lapping of waves as they gently break onto the shore; the wind rustling through the fall trees; the sensation of your own breathing as it gently goes in and out), you can't *not* think about the images associated with the thoughts that you are processing. And because we can only actively process one thought at a time, while we are counting sheep we cannot be processing the thoughts and images that cause us worry at the same time. These thoughts are neutral and relaxing and because they help direct your mind to find that peaceful place, you will find it easier to fall asleep. It takes mental control, but the strategy is foolproof, and with practice, you can learn to deliberately quiet your mind.

CHAPTER 8

RULE #4

Your *Dominant Thought* Determines Your Emotions, the Behaviors that Flow from Those Emotions, and Ultimately Your Ability to Perform

It's not what you look at that matters,
it's what you see.

—HENRY DAVID THOREAU, ESSAYIST, POET, & PHILOSOPHER

 Because we think in pictures, whatever we process in our mind as a dominant thought has a direct influence on our feelings, the behaviors that result from those feelings, and ultimately on our ability to perform.

I recognize that this is a bold statement, but if you consider the basic principles regarding imagery that we discussed earlier, together with the pendulum exercise, it is not so hard to believe that when we vividly imagine ourselves feeling or performing in a certain way, our body adjusts to act on that information. For example, when we watch a frightening movie, our heart begins to race, our muscles become tense, and our breathing speeds up. When we watch a hilarious comedy, we laugh and our mood brightens. When we watch a sad movie, we become sad and may even cry.

The events taking place before us are not real and yet, when we imagine ourselves in these different scenarios by viewing them on a screen, our body and mind behave in much the same way as they would if we were truly there, albeit at a lower level of intensity. Recall the analogy of the dimmer switch when I explained why the pendulum moves the way that it does.

But how or why does this occur? Understanding the why of this process depends upon understanding the basic difference that exists between your conscious and your unconscious mind. The conscious part of our mind is the rational, objective, discriminating faculty of the brain. Its role is to take in information from our environment, compare it with our previous experiences, determine whether it is relevant or not, then finally make a decision. Every single piece of information that our conscious mind accepts is then accepted by our unconscious mind as well. It is accepted as being true, as fact, even though it may or may not reflect reality accurately.

 In other words, your unconscious mind does not dispute the accuracy or validity of the information you process within your conscious mind, it accepts it without debate as being fundamentally true, acts accordingly, and what is more significant, *you cannot directly control it.*

If I command you right now to be happy, can you do it? Or if I ask you to be sad at this very moment in time, would you be able to? Obviously, as I stated previously, you could not. We cannot directly control our emotions. They evolve as a result of the thought processes that take place in our conscious mind. The only way to feel true happiness is to consciously think "happy thoughts," and the more vividly we process those happy thoughts, the more a happy or joyous mind-set evolves within us. Likewise, the only way to feel deep sadness is to think sad thoughts in our conscious mind, and if we are able to do so with conviction, we gradually become more and more sad and soon we become over-whelmed with sorrow.

Our conscious mind is like the captain of a ship that sets the direction. The unconscious mind then seeks to implement that direction, to act like the crew and follow the captain's orders with-out debate or reservation. Think back to the mechanism of action at work during the pendulum exercise we discussed in Chapter 3.

Rule #4 simply affirms that our dominant mind-set directly affects our ability to perform. Each of us, regardless of our age, has more than likely experienced the consequences of this powerful rule in the real world. Consider the following:

- Circumstances or belief systems that lead us to become afraid, to develop feelings of anxiety with its associated physical tension, often deny us the ability to focus effectively on a task . . . and our performance is not as good as it might have been.

- Situations in which we feel a high degree of motivation and desire seem to allow us unlimited reserves of energy and strength.

- A loss of confidence creates periods of self-doubt where images of failure become self-fulfilling prophecies that infect and poison our feelings, behaviors, and ultimately, our performance.

- Environments that allow us to remain calm and focused usually allow us to generate and deliver our best personal performances.

Every one of us always acts, feels, and behaves in a way that is consistent with our own self-image, regardless of the reality or accuracy of that image. We act and feel not according to what things are really like, but according to the image our mind holds of what they are like, and the truth is that we acquire our self-image through unconscious habit. While it is not *easy* to change such a habit, it is *simple* enough. It just takes repeated practice implementing a new, hopefully better habit.

Positive and productive dominant thoughts generally preface our best performances, while negative and counterproductive dominant thoughts lead to anxiety, loss of appropriate focus, and poor performance. We can use this fundamental truth about the human mind to help ourselves perform to the best of our ability on command, rather than to sabotage ourselves through negative thinking that draws our focus away from the task in front of us. This truth serves as the basis of the A.C.T. Model© process we will discuss in the final section of this book.

CHAPTER 9

RULE #5

You *Are* in Control
of Your Dominant Thought

God, grant me the serenity to accept the things I cannot change,
courage to change the things that I can,
and wisdom to know the difference.

—REINHOLD NIEBUHR, THEOLOGIAN

Knowing is not enough, we must apply.
Willing is not enough, we must do.

—JOHANN WOLFGANG VON GOETHE, WRITER, ARTIST, & BIOLOGIST

We are still masters of our fate.
We are still captains of our soul.

—WINSTON CHURCHILL, POLITICIAN & STATESMAN

There are so many things in life over which we have little or no control. There is, however, one thing over which you can learn to have greater and greater control—your mind. Many people do not understand that you *choose* what you believe. Each of your beliefs is a choice that you have made at some point in your life. Our tendency is to allow in only information that conforms to our innermost beliefs, whether these beliefs are consistent with reality or not, and to reject information that does not conform to those fundamental beliefs.

The most damaging effect on you and your performance comes from beliefs you hold strongly about yourself and your inability to successfully engage and even accomplish the challenges you choose to take on. These self-limiting beliefs then naturally and automatically lead to self-limiting behaviors, because your focus shifts to the many worries you have and the fear that you might not succeed, rather than to the task in front of you. The fundamental problem seems relatively simple to understand, but the solution is not quite so easy to implement. The solution starts with the ability to control your own mind.

 If you learn how to control your dominant thought such that your mind consistently sees what it is that you want and what you want to be like when you perform with excellence, your personal performance in anything that you undertake will be the best that it can be given the skills, knowledge, and abilities you possess at that moment in time.

Your abilities will be applied fully to the task you are focused on and you will deny your central processor the capacity and the opportunity to create the self-sabotaging mind-set that so often infects our performance in those moments when we face our greatest challenges. We cannot control the outcome, but we can ensure with this kind of thinking that we bring our "A" game to the performance (the process), whatever it is that we are doing. We leave nothing on the table!

The problem is that each of us often simply fails to recognize that we have control in the first place; and then secondly, we systematically fail to exercise it. So often, we allow the environment around us and the situations and challenges that we face to dictate our dominant thought. We bounce off our environmental circumstances, and our dominant thought ends up being defined within those events, rather than by us exercising control over our mind as we face those events. Furthermore, when we feel like we are out of control, anxiety spikes and it affects our performance in a negative way.

You can learn to control your dominant thought and by doing so effectively choose the tint of the filter—or the rose-colored glasses—through which you interpret the challenges and opportunities of your life. You can become the boss of your own mind, and if you do so in a conscious and systematic way, you will establish a mind-set that allows you to more consistently deliver your best performances on command. The rub, of course, is in knowing how to do it, and the A.C.T. Model© process will provide you with a defined starting point to accomplish this very task.

CHAPTER 10

RULE #6

Your *Perception* or *Perspective* Regarding the Challenges You Face Will Determine Your Emotional Response

Men are disturbed not by events,
but by the views which they take of them.
—EPICTETUS, GREEK PHILOSOPHER

Whether you think you can or you can't, you're right.
—HENRY FORD, BUSINESS LEADER

In the 1950s, Dr. Albert Ellis, a world-renowned clinical psychologist and author founded a model of cognitive behavioral therapy that he called "rational emotive behavior therapy." The basic tenet of this form of therapy is that whenever we become upset or stressed out, it is not the events taking place in our life at that time that are causing the stress but rather, that the stress response is a direct result of the belief we hold with respect to that event. To put it another way, it is not the events in our life that cause us stress. It is our perception or interpretation of those events that leads to a stress response that on the one hand, can be negative and counterproductive for our health and performance, or on the other hand, can be positive and contribute to our health and our ability to perform.

Dr. Ellis framed this relationship by developing a simple A-B-C paradigm where "A" leads to "B," which then in turn leads to "C." In the paradigm he outlined, "A" does not lead to "C" directly; it *always* goes through "B":

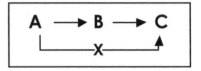

Dr. Ellis defined the A-B-C variables as follows:

"A" is the *activating event*—the situation or event that we are reacting to. Often, this event is outside of our direct control since it may be imposed on us by others or by circumstances in our environment.

"B" is our *belief* with respect to that event—something that is fully within our control to change or adapt, assuming of course that we choose to exercise that control.

"C" represents the *consequences* of that belief. Again, this is something that is outside of our direct control since these consequences, our emotions, are automatically defined by our unconscious mind in response to our conscious thoughts and beliefs.

Let me give you a couple of concrete examples to illustrate this point: Example #1 comes from the world of business, while Example #2 comes from the world of motor racing:

Example #1: Two salesmen from competing companies arrive at a local hotel because each is scheduled to make a major sales presentation to prospective buyers from one of the leading companies in their industry. Initially, they were to meet with the vice president for sales only, but ten minutes prior to their presentation, each is told that not only will the VP for sales be present, but so too will two other senior VPs for marketing and finance, as well as the president of the company. The deal they are to discuss has just recently escalated in importance and volume, and because it could be so financially significant, all of these key executives want to be able to ask the questions that they feel are important to satisfy their individual concerns.

Salesman #1 thinks to himself: "Good grief, what am I going to do? I've only got a half-hour to answer all of their questions! I will never be able to satisfy their need for information in that short a time. Not only that, I know that most of these people don't really understand the processes that our company uses, and I am afraid that I won't be able to convince them that our company's product is their best choice. I never do well in these kinds of high-pressure situations. I get so nervous that I trip over my tongue every time! I just can't seem to get comfortable. Why did these other guys have to show up? This meeting is going to be a disaster! What will my boss think?"

When faced with the same information, salesman #2 thinks to himself: "Good grief, what a great opportunity!! It is so tough to get all of the key decision makers to focus on one thing at the same time, and I have them all in the same room for thirty minutes. I know they won't expect to get all the details in that short a time. My job is to excite them about this opportunity for collaboration and show them that our company's product and reputation is their best option. I always do well when the challenge in front of me is well defined! These people put their pants on one leg at a time just like I do and I know I can deliver the goods. What a lucky break! I can't wait to get in there to show them what we can do as a company to help make them more successful! The boss is going to love this!!"

Assuming the quality of their product or service is equal, it should be obvious which salesman is going to be more effective and is more likely to bring home the big contract. Let us go back to our A-B-C explanation to better understand this scenario.

The activating event—the "A" in this scenario—is the same for both individuals: ten minutes prior to their scheduled meeting, each is informed that other key players will be participating.

Their belief about the event (the "B" in the perception paradigm) is quite different however! Salesman #1 sees the change of plans as a threat, with the arrival of company heavyweights as a sign of doom and disaster. Salesman #2, on the other hand, sees the change as a positive, a situation that could turn to his advantage and make closing the big deal that much easier because he is being provided with the opportunity to make his presentation to all of the key players at the same time.

What are the consequences (the "C" in our paradigm) that each will realize as a result of their beliefs? Salesman #1 will likely become anxious and physically tense as the meeting approaches, and the increased tension will cause him to narrow his focus and lose the mental flexibility needed to think on his feet. He will likely be overly concerned with the consequences of a "sales pitch gone wrong," and he may very well become tongue-tied, just the way he pictured it in his mind! His anxiety and lack of confidence will be observed by the others in the room, and they will begin to wonder whether this individual believes in what he is selling. Salesman #2, on the other hand, becomes energized by the thought of hitting a home run and enters the room more relaxed, confident, and mentally sharp. He will likely be more effective at delivering a clear overview of the value proposition for his product, and his easy and professional manner will have a positive impact on his audience.

Now let us consider the second example:

Example #2: On the morning of race day, two motor racing drivers wake up to their alarm and move to the window of their respective hotel rooms. They pull the curtain open and note that the sky is grey and there is a light rain falling.

Driver #1 sees the cloudy and rainy conditions and says to himself: "Darn, why did it have to rain today! I never do well in wet conditions. In fact, in the last three races in the wet, I've crashed the car. I get so anxious when the track is wet that I can't seem to find any rhythm in the car. I worry so much about messing up. Why did it have to rain? It's going to be a terrible day."

On the other hand, Driver #2 thinks to himself: "Great, it's raining today! Finally, I'll get the chance to show my competitors and all the team owners what I can do when the playing field is level.

Our car is down on power compared to the big-budget teams but the rain is an equalizer. Now it's not about power, it's about car control skills and I have great car control skills. I've always done well in the wet and today will be my opportunity to shine. Bring it on!"

The activating event ("A") is the same in both cases: the sky is grey and there is a light rain falling. Driver #1 believes ("B") that the event spells gloom and doom for him, and his fear and negative expectation have a greater chance of becoming a self-fulfilling prophecy as his unconscious mind begins to act on his negative conscious thoughts and images ("C"). He becomes physically tense and his focus of attention is redirected from performance-relevant thoughts to thoughts of failure and the fear of negative outcomes.

For Driver #2, the same event is viewed as an opportunity to shine, to demonstrate his skill in a way that he is not able to do in other situations when the track is dry, because he is limited by budget and a lower power engine. Who do you believe is going to be more effective in this scenario? If we consider for just a moment how Rule #4 (the dominant thought rule) informs our response, it is quite obvious that the mind-set adopted by driver #2 is likely to optimize his performance whereas the mind-set adopted by driver #1 will likely corrupt his performance by causing him to focus on the wrong things, such as picturing himself crashing the car, and the pendulum *will* move.

I could use many more examples to illustrate this point but I am confident that you have thought about examples in your own life where this basic rule has held up well. What is the impact of Rule #6 on performance? Here it is: realize that in our A-B-C paradigm, "A" always leads to "B," which in turn always leads to "C."

 "A," the activating event does *not* lead directly to "C," the consequences! It is always your beliefs, your perceptions regarding the activating events in your life, that lead to the consequences that you ultimately experience.

The beauty and the power of this realization is that if you change your belief about the activating events in your life, you will change the consequences that you experience, *because your unconscious mind will accept this new perception as being real.* This is something that is 100 percent within your control to do, since Rule #5 states that we *are* in control of our dominant thought. It is simple enough to understand as a conceptual framework, it just is not very easy to apply consistently in the real world.

What I would like to do now is to shift our discussion to touch on some additional background information that I believe is important to consider. The information that I would like to focus on now deals with the topic of stress and our ability to cope with it, anxiety and its influence on performance, and the relationship between anxiety, confidence, and focus. This information will provide context to help you to better understand where Rule #6 comes from and the power that this simple rule can have in your life. While it may represent a different way of looking at things, I hope that you will be open to considering a different perspective regarding what actually causes stress, and your ability to more effectively deal with it.

As we begin this shift in focus, I would like you to consider the following statements and place a pencil mark across the line between the two boxes that identifies where you believe that you fall with respect to the thoughts identified in each statement. A mark close to the **"MAX"** end of the line means that you agree completely with the particular statement, and a mark close to **"MIN"** end of the line means that you do not agree at all with the statement as it relates to your life and your situation. There are no correct or incorrect answers here so just be honest with yourself and provide the best estimate you can of your feelings with respect to your situation and beliefs.

To what degree do you feel that you have personal control over your own thoughts, emotions, and behaviors, as well as over the activities in which you engage? How well do you feel that you are the "boss" of your own mind?

To what degree do you feel that you are an important part of your work and life interactions, enjoying the activities that you are involved with and fully engaged in them? How committed are you to the path you are walking in your life at this moment?

To what degree do you generally view changes in your life (whether you judge these changes to be positive or negative) as a positive challenge or opportunity? To what extent do you see new situations as opportunities to grow and measure yourself against that challenge?

What degree of emotional and mental support do you feel you have with respect to problems or difficulties that you may confront in your life (both in work and in your personal life)? This statement reflects the human/emotional connections you feel that you can count on for support when the situation you are facing becomes very difficult or challenging.

We will come back to this exercise a little later on as we begin to discuss the issue of how we cope with stress.

It is safe to say that humans are creatures of habit. We tend to be comfortable with routine and for the most part, do not manage change very well. In fact, the vast majority of people find change inherently to be stressful, and the more change we have going on in our life, the more stress we seem to feel. Over the years, researchers have sought to understand how change itself is associated with health. Many clinicians have observed that the more a patient reflects a family history of ongoing significant upheaval (that is, change), the more the individual seems to wrestle with health issues. Intuitively, I suspect that this makes sense to most of us.

In an attempt to study this relationship more fully, in 1967 two psychiatrists by the name of Thomas Holmes and Richard Rahe created a questionnaire that sought to quantify how much change was going on in a person's life, and studied whether the amount of change people were dealing with was, or was not, related to their health status. They compared the responses from more than 5,000 patients on their Social Readjustment Rating Scale (which has also commonly been called the Life Change Events Scale) against their medical history, to determine what the nature of the relationship was between these two variables.

What they found in general was that, indeed, the amount of change that a person was dealing with in their life, as a *cumulative* variable, seems to have a direct effect on their health status. The greater the amount of life change the individual was wrestling with, the greater was the potential negative impact on their health. There was a strong relationship established between "life change events" and negative health consequences, and if you look at the two black rectangles in Figure 15, you can think of them as movable sliders that seem to be tied together. This is based simply on the proven relationship that exists between life change and health. Note that the levels used in these figures are for illustration purposes only.

What this work effectively says is that the more change we have going on in our life, the greater the potential exists for negative health consequences. Interestingly, it does not mean that the change in question is necessarily negative, since the Holmes/Rahe Social Readjustment Rating Scale lists a number of change events

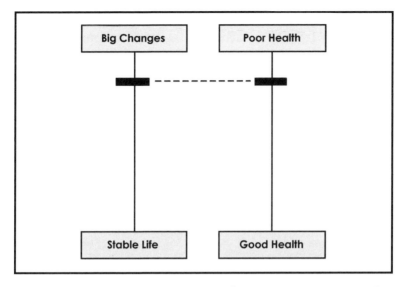

FIGURE 15. The Relationship Between Life Change Events and Health Status

that would be considered by most individuals to be positive in their life—for example: marriage, the birth of a child, beginning school, outstanding personal achievement, going on vacation or experiencing major holidays like Christmas, and so forth. These are events in a person's life that, while positive, can still be quite stressful because they represent a meaningful change in the status quo. Anyone who has experienced the birth of a child will readily understand this perspective.

On the flip side, when there is not a lot of change going on in our life, the research suggests that this more stable life situation bodes well for good health. In short, the higher the aggregate score on the Holmes/Rahe scale, the greater the risk for negative health consequences, while the lower the aggregate score on the scale, the less there appears to be a risk of illness. While the data may seem to suggest that this relationship is straightforward, is the situation actually this simple? Not really.

The issue revolves around the mental state of negative arousal that we call "stress." The health consequences we experience are generally accepted as being directly related to the level of negative stress that we feel. It is well recognized today that the hypothala-mus-pituitary-adrenal interaction in the brain responds to stress by releasing high concentrations of a hormone called cortisol into our body. Prolonged exposure to stressful circumstances—and corti-sol—can produce long-lasting effects on physical and mental health and, given our particular interest, on performance as well, because of the long-term impact of cortisol on body systems. So the picture evolves to take on a slightly different look as outlined in Figure 16.

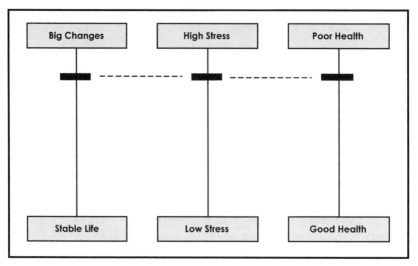

FIGURE 16. The Intermediary of Stress in the Life Change / Health Equation

It now appears that we should introduce into our thinking an intervening variable in the life change-health relationship that helps to explain *why* change (both positive and negative) seems to be so tightly related to health status. The equation again appears simple enough: a large amount of life change is normally associated for most people with a high degree of stress, which in turn influences the body systems to facilitate the development of illness. Intuitively, I do not think that many of us will disagree with this logic. But again, we have to ask ourselves the question: "Is it really this straightforward?" And again, the answer is: not really.

Why is it that some people who are exposed to significant life change events crumble emotionally and physically, and why does the stress often associated with events such as the battle with a major disease cause them to succumb, while others do not? What is it that differentiates individuals who seem to be more stress-susceptible from others who seem to be stress-resistant? Researchers often refer to this latter kind of person as being "stress hardy."

 If we examine the extensive pool of research that seeks to understand the fundamental difference between the stress-resistant and stress-susceptible individual, it seems that the secret lies in large part in their ability to more effectively *cope* with the stressful situation that they are dealing with.

Stated another way, there seems to be an inverse relationship between coping skills and negative stress such that, when coping skills are strong, the negative stress response is muted, but when coping skills are weak, negative stress tends to be greater. We now must introduce the variable of *coping ability* into our illustration. Coping skills, or lack thereof, seem to account for much of the difference between these two types of individuals, and when coping skills are poor, especially when there are big life changes afoot, the elevated negative stress response often leads to poor health, as illustrated in Figure 17.

When coping skills are weak but there are not a lot of life changes to deal with, the stress response tends to be low as well because we are not called upon to adapt to or cope with much of anything. But when life-change events spike as they always do, since one of the greatest constants in life is that *things will change,* poor coping skills do not allow the stress-susceptible individual much protection.

On the other hand, when the stress-resistant individual

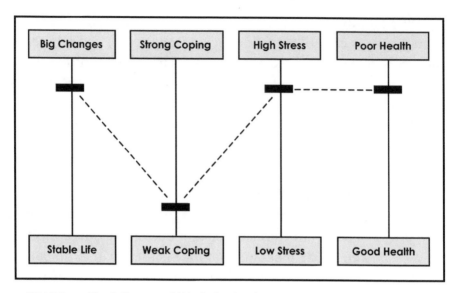

FIGURE 17. The Influence of Weak Coping Skills on Stress and Health Status

encounters a great deal of life-change events, their ability to effectively cope with the upheaval that those events bring yields a low negative stress response. As we might expect, they also seem to have a lower risk of illness in these situations (as outlined in Figure 18). This simple explanation ties together a number of key components: the pressures that life throws at us, how we mentally cope with them, the stress response that is subsequently generated within us, and the effect of that stress response on both our health and performance.

Since our ability to cope with stress seems to be a critical variable in this mix, let us now consider what defines our ability to cope effectively with stress. The research, although extensive and conducted over many years, suggests that the core of our coping skills can be described by four simple variables, not unlike the parts of a four-legged stool (with our set of coping skills being the metaphorical seat of the stool): our sense of *control*; our level of *commitment*; how we view *change*; and the level of emotional *connections* or support that we feel we have from important people in our life.

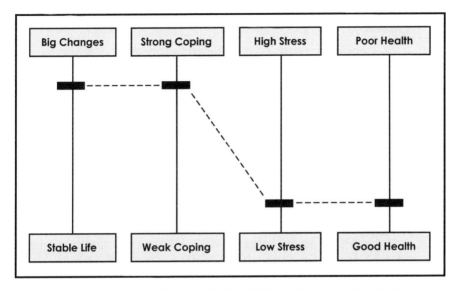

FIGURE 18. The Impact of Strong Coping Skills on Stress and Health Status

I would like to refer back now to the MIN/MAX exercise that I asked you to complete earlier in this chapter, where you placed a mark across the line to describe how you felt about the statements associated with each line. In a nutshell, the more to the right you placed your mark on each line, the more that mark signals a tendency to be stress-resistant. The more to the left you placed your mark, the more stress-susceptible you tend to be. Let me repeat each statement of that exercise to make it easier to discuss them in turn.

Sense of Control

To what degree do you feel that you have personal control over your own thoughts, emotions, and behaviors, as well as over the activities in which you engage? How well do you feel you are the "boss" of your own mind?

| MIN | ———————————————— | MAX |

The vast body of research essentially tells us that individuals who understand that they cannot control what they cannot control (the "B" factors in life), but who recognize that they have complete control over how they choose to see those events, are automatically more stress-resistant than those who have the opposite perspective.

The stress-resistant individual feels that they are in control of their own thoughts and to a large degree, are the masters of their own destiny. Their sense of control allows them to more calmly and systematically engage the challenge in front of them and as a result, they tend to focus more on their actions rather than on the consequences of failure.

Individuals who put their mark toward the left side of the line tend to feel more out of control. They perceive themselves as victims with little sense of control of their own destiny. They are a caboose on the freight train of life that is dragging them along with no perceived sense of meaningful personal control.

The research tells us that individuals who tend to feel victimized are more stress-susceptible. They tend to focus most of their energy and thoughts on their failure to control things (which they actually cannot control for the most part), and on the negative situation that they are in. They stare at their shoes, digging madly, all the while worrying about whether they will ever get out of the mental and emotional hole that they are in. A sense of powerlessness is thought of as being a major contributing factor in the heightened negative stress response. Coping resources can compensate for the potentially crippling effects of stressful events, and the construct of psychological hardiness is thought to buffer the negative effects of stress.

Coping is a dynamic process that essentially involves us interacting with and adjusting to our environmental circumstances, and a strong sense of control signals a positive, adaptive coping strategy that usually presents itself in one of two ways:

Problem-focused coping strategies. With this type of strategy, individuals do something active and constructive in the face of the challenge they must deal with. They take control of their own actions and thought processes as they become the "boss" of their own mind and choose to act to try to resolve their problem. Their focus turns to the steps that they can take to make things better rather than constantly just worrying about—and complaining about—the fact that things are not good. Men often seem to naturally lean in this direction and adopt this strategy; they tend to try to "fix" the situation.

Emotion-focused coping strategies. This strategy, while more passive, is directed toward gaining emotional control and understanding about the stressful event. Women generally seem to lean in this direction. They tend to "vent" about the situation, try to understand it and come to terms with it. As they become successful in coming to terms with the issue, their perspective changes and they grow to more effectively cope with the problem.

Where on the line did you put your mark?

Sense of Commitment

To what degree do you feel that you are an important part of your work and life interactions, enjoying the activities that you are involved with and fully engaged in them? How committed are you to the path you are walking in your life at this moment?

The second component of our coping skill tool kit revolves around the issue of commitment. Simply put, the more committed we are to the path we have chosen in our life, the more stress-resistant we automatically become. The less we are committed to move in a clear direction to achieve the goals we have set for ourselves, the more easily we are derailed from the actions that will lead us to those goals. As a consequence, the more stress-susceptible we become.

Here is how I often describe this component of our stress-coping tool kit: We are heading down life's path and we encounter a pothole—a challenging situation or life event. The pothole in question could be a serious disease, a financial setback, a difficult performance issue, and so on. If we are committed to the target we are heading toward at the end of the path, if the goal burns brightly in our mind, we view the pothole or problem simply as an obstacle that we must navigate on the way to our goal. This commitment fuels our perseverance, and more often than not, by diligently working at finding a solution, we overcome the obstacle in question and we continue our progress down the road. In your experience, how often does it happen that as you glance in the rearview mirror of your life and reflect on the obstacles you have been successful in overcoming, that you come to realize that it was often not as bad as you thought it was going to be at the time. The committed individual is simply more stress-resistant in the face of life's many challenges.

The individual who is not fully committed on the other hand, has a vastly different perspective on the pothole that life puts in his way. Because the goal at the end of the road does not burn brightly, he is less likely to persevere in the face of that obstacle. He is more likely to give up because he believes that the pothole represents an insurmountable obstacle and that there is no way that he can get beyond it successfully.

The pothole becomes a *barrier* that prevents further progress instead of simply being an obstacle to be navigated, and his unconscious mind accepts that belief as reality.

Commitment is an important tool in our coping skills tool kit, and it comes totally from within. It cannot be imposed upon us by someone else. We, and only we, make the decision to be fully committed or not. The choice we make, however, has an effect on how stress-resistant or -susceptible we are and ultimately, on our health and performance as well. Where on the line did you put your mark?

How We View Change

To what degree do you generally view changes in your life (whether you judge these changes to be positive or negative at the time) as a positive challenge or opportunity? To what extent do you see new situations as opportunities to grow and measure yourself against that challenge?

The relationship between life changes and health brought to light through the work of Holmes and Rahe informs us that we the people do not "do change" very well as a general rule! That is why the magnitude of life change events is so closely related to health status. Research tells us that the individual who accepts that change is an integral part of life, and indeed one of its greatest constants, and who purposefully looks for the opportunity that change most often brings, is automatically more stress-resistant than the individual who constantly and tenaciously pushes back against change.

This does not mean that we must like the change that is happening but rather, when it is forced upon us by circumstances outside of our control, that we accept it as part of life and try to make the most out of a changing situation. The individual who rails against change and resists it with every fiber of their being is automatically more stress-susceptible when change is thrust upon them. They become angry, depressed, disillusioned, and incorrectly focused, and their negative emotional state prevents them from moving on and tackling the problem with a more optimistic, positive, and task-focused mind-set. Their negative perspective drives the negative emotional stress that they feel, and the systems within their body react to the negative effects of anxiety. The cortisol response is triggered and their health and performance is more likely to deteriorate. Where on the line did you put your mark?

Sense of Connections

What degree of emotional and mental support do you feel you have with respect to problems or difficulties that you may confront in your life (both in work and in your personal life)? This statement reflects the human/emotional connections you feel that you can count on for support when the situation you are facing becomes very difficult or challenging.

The last component in our coping skills tool kit revolves around the sense of emotional support or connection that we feel with people around us. The more you feel "connected"—that is, the more to the right you put your mark on the line—the more stress-resistant you automatically tend to be. The less you feel you have emotional support when faced with a major life challenge, the more stress-susceptible you tend to be. The interesting thing about this component is that we do not have to enjoy support from a great many people, but rather that we feel a deep-rooted emotional support from someone in our life: a parent, a sibling, a spouse, a child, a coworker, a teammate, a classmate, a friend. It reflects the degree to which we feel that we have someone who will backstop us if we end up in a difficult situation where we need emotional support. If we have a pool of such people with whom we enjoy this kind of support, we find it much easier to be stress-resistant than if we feel that we are alone, that if something happens to us and we end up in difficulty, we are on our own.

Here is the way that I would describe it: We are walking along the tightrope of life, taking steps cautiously because some of the challenges we face are significant. If we look down and see a strong, robust safety net below that is there to catch us should we fall, we are able to more effectively remain calm, with less fear, and focus on taking each step to the best of our ability. We trust that if circumstances cause us to fall, we will have the necessary emotional support we need to get back up on the wire and re-engage the challenge in front of us. If, on the other hand, we look down from that high wire and only see the concrete floor, because we do not believe that we have an emotional safety net to rely on, our fear of falling and its consequences increases, and we become unable to take the steps that will lead us along our path. In this situation, we might even picture ourselves falling, and our fears become crippling as we freeze in place. We become incapable of taking the steps necessary to move on. Remember the example of the twenty-five-foot board we discussed on page 62 in the section about imagery.

The sad irony that underpins the very existence of our coping skills is that reality does not really matter in the situations that I have outlined above. For each of the four coping variables we have discussed, it is not the reality of the situation that either causes us stress or reduces our negative stress response, but rather it is our *perception* of that situation that informs our stress response (the heart of Rule #6).

Let me share with you some information that should help to put this basic principle into context.

Over the years, I have found myself on many occasions conducting Team Performance seminars with groups of individuals from NASCAR and Open Wheel race teams who compete at the highest levels of the competitive world in their form of racing. The individuals participating in these programs include technical and management personnel as well as pit crew members who go over the wall repeatedly during a race to service their team's car (tires, gas, and so forth).

As part of these seminar programs, I ask each participant to complete some preseminar questionnaires so that the confidential analysis of this data can give them a sense of their personal situation as I discuss various performance-relevant topics with the group. One of the things that I am interested in examining is the relationship between the amount of change that they have going on in their life and the strength of the coping skills they possess to effectively deal with these potentially stressful situations. I am interested in this because I want to understand what the level of external distraction is that they must contend with as they seek to deliver their best performance within their competitive environment. I will share with you the profile of two individuals from different teams that will shed some light on how this relationship translates in the real world.

The Holmes/Rahe Life Change Events Scale allows us to calculate an aggregate or cumulative score that represents the amount of life change that an individual has faced over the year preceding the completion of the questionnaire. A score of less than 150 signals a relatively stable life, which bodes well for a low likelihood of illness, while an aggregate score of 300 or above signals significant life change with a correspondingly high potential for illness. The two highest scores I have ever encountered in any of my client populations using this scale are 870 and 852! Needless to say, they had a *lot* of stuff going on in their life, and the simple relationship demonstrated by the Holmes/Rahe work suggests that both of these individuals are accidents waiting to happen! Their health should be at risk and their performance should be subpar to say the least. Note that I also had them complete a number of other questionnaires that give me an even clearer picture of their stress/anxiety pre-disposition, since none of these questionnaires by themselves give us the full picture of a person and the situational factors that they are dealing with.

The coping skills assessment tool that I utilize in these situations allows us to create an aggregate score that ranges from 0 to 100, reflecting the overall effectiveness of an individual's coping skills. The higher the aggregate score, the better seems to be their coping ability—that is, the more to the right they tend to *honestly* put their mark on the line—while the lower the score, the more they seem to struggle to cope with the upheaval going on in their life in that window of time. The scores for the two individuals described above were 98 and 35, respectively. I spent some time with these two individuals after the seminars to find out more about their situation and to offer some perspective.

Individual #1 scored **870** on the life change scale and **98** on the coping scale. If I was to put this profile, without identifying the person it came from, in front of members of this individual's team and ask them who they thought it might be, never in a month of Sundays would they identify the individual in question. He is one of the most productive and focused individuals in the organization, and his performance is never in question. He had a lot on his plate during this time but had an exceptional ability to cope with what was going on. His mind-set seemed to generally be positive and task-focused. His health also appears to be good, even though he is a little older than some of his teammates.

Individual #2 scored **852** on the life change scale and **35** on the coping scale. After talking with this individual, I suggested that he might want to speak with a professional counselor because he was really struggling with an inability to cope with the many significant things that he was trying to deal with in his life. I cautioned him that if he did not find a way to more effectively deal with these issues, it would affect his health and his performance in a negative way. He broke down and acknowledged that he had been to see the doctor in the previous week; he was told that he had a heart condition and was showing signs of diabetes. He also acknowledged that it was affecting his work as he was making more mistakes because he was distracted/preoccupied by his situation and everything that he was trying to deal with. I am glad to report that he took my advice and when I spoke with him several months later, he informed me that things were going much better both on the health and the work side of the equation, as he felt that he was getting a good grip on things and was turning the corner.

The point of this real-world example is simply to reinforce the basic principle that it is not the activating events in our life that cause us negative stress and corrupt our health and performance, but rather, it is more about how we choose to see these things—how we cope with them—that has the greatest effect on our health and performance. If we maintain a negative mind-set, we become distracted and focus on the things that are worrying us, and our level of stress increases. The more effectively we can cope with stress, the more we can remain correctly focused and perform to our highest level of ability.

I would like to turn our attention now to discuss what the world of psychology refers to as *trait anxiety*. Trait anxiety refers to the predisposition that each of us has to be more or less anxious as a general tendency. Some people, as a character trait, given their current situation and the perspective they adopt about it, tend to be more trait anxious (often referred to as high responders), while others tend to be less so (considered low responders). The more trait-anxious person feels things deeply and quickly. They are emotionally reactive and they "rev up" with little provocation. This does not mean that they always show it, because sometimes they work very hard to hide their feelings; but it does mean that they feel it deeply and easily. When things are good, we have to peel the high responder off the ceiling, but when things are bad, we have to dig them out of the subbasement! Their range of emotional volatility is broad, and they tend to swing from highs to lows more easily than less trait-anxious individuals.

The less anxious person reacts to things very differently. It almost seems that we have to beat on these people with a stick to get a rise out of them. We see two very different responses to the same kind of situation. These individuals are certainly capable of highs and lows, but the responses are more muted. When things are good they tend to think, "That's great, but let's not go crazy." But when things are bad, they tend to think, "That sucks, but let's not get carried away." Their emotional volatility swings in a less dramatic fashion.

What does the performance literature suggest about these two individuals? In essence, the information from the performance world informs us that the low-responder mind-set is more conducive to high performance while the high-responder mind-set is less likely to be associated with championship-caliber performance. Ultimately, I believe that it comes back to the holy grail of the performance equation—to the issue of *correct focus*!

The high responder has such a broad emotional volatility that it is very difficult for these individuals to bring their focus to bear on specific things and control it to be directed to the right thing at the right time, for any length of time. Their inability to sustain their focus of attention on performance-relevant thoughts and actions means that all too often they are focused on the wrong thing, and their performance deteriorates accordingly. The low responder, on the other hand, has a much narrower range of emotional volatility, and it is much easier for that individual to control and indeed sustain their focus of attention to be on the right thing at the right time. They are not as easily pulled off task by the external and internal distracters in their environment, and their correct focus usually translates to better performance and better results.

Can we change our trait anxiety predisposition? I can tell you without equivocation that we can, because I have observed such a shift in thinking in many of my clients over the years. It is simple enough in principle, although it is not totally easy in practice. In a nutshell, we can accomplish this shift in our trait anxiety predisposition by doing a better job of policing our thoughts and controlling our perspective on the many challenging situations that we encounter in life.

 If we become better at *eavesdropping* on our own internal mind chatter and adjusting, in some cases even challenging, our thought processes to focus more effectively on that which we can truly control (our own "A" game), we stop worrying about the "B" factors in life or about results.

As we accomplish this, the shift occurs naturally and relatively easily. It is not as difficult as you might think. The A.C.T. Model© (discussed in detail in Part Three) will explain how you can begin to move down this path.

Learned Helplessness vs. Learned Optimism

In the early 1960s, noted psychologist Dr. Martin Seligman and his associate Steven Maier developed the concept that ultimately became known as "learned helplessness." Their work was an outgrowth of an interest in studying the phenomenon of depression, to understand what causes individuals to suffer with this crippling and all-too-frequent condition that seems to be growing into an epidemic in today's society.

It appears that the perception of lack of control in someone's life is a common thread that underpins the state of emotional depression from which many people suffer. They believe that the problems they are facing are insurmountable, pervasive, permanent, and that it is their fault. In his book *Learned Optimism* (see the Recommended Reading section at the end of the book), Dr. Seligman states:

"The defining characteristics of pessimists is that they tend to believe bad events will last a long time, will undermine every-thing they do, and are their own fault. The optimists who are confronted with the same hard knocks of this world, think about misfortune in the opposite way. They tend to believe defeat is just a temporary setback, that its causes are confined to this one case. [They] believe defeat is not their fault: Cir-cumstances, bad luck, or other people brought it about. Such people are unfazed by defeat. Confronted by a bad situation, they perceive it as a challenge and try harder . . ."

There are literally hundreds of studies that suggest that pes-simists give up more easily and get depressed more often than do optimists, and research reinforces the fact that optimists do much better in school, are more effective at work and on the playing field, and so forth.

I would like to put this concept into terms that we can all understand more easily by citing a couple of examples that Dr. Seligman references in his books. I found that they summarize the fundamental precepts of the learned helplessness model in a sim-ple, graphic way:

Circus example. When a baby elephant is born into the circus, the elephant trainer tethers the elephant to a chain that is attached to a stake driven into the ground within the elephant enclosure. The purpose of this restraint is to teach the elephant to remain in its enclosure, and when it is small, the chain actually prevents it from wandering outside of the relatively restrictive space defined by the length of its chain. The baby elephant pulls on the chain but it cannot escape its confines because it is limited by that restraint. It effectively learns that pulling on the chain is futile and that its confinement to a small enclosure is a permanent condition of its life. Over a relatively brief amount of time, it stops pulling on the chain altogether. It comes to accept an internal representation of itself as a captive creature that is incapable of breaking free, and it continues to reflect this belief in its behavior. As it grows to become a full-size elephant, the elephant does not pull on the chain because it has learned that it is futile, even though it could pull the stake out of the ground with ease as a full-grown elephant!

Aquarium example. When a city aquarium was looking to create a new marine exhibit that featured large, somewhat aggressive game fish, it ran into a problem. As the marine biologists sought to introduce smaller fish into the exhibit to fill out the natural ecosystem, it was like ringing the dinner bell. As soon as the small fish were introduced into the tank, the bigger fish treated them like a meal, and the biologists could not keep small fish in the tank because they would constantly get eaten!

One enterprising individual thought of a creative solution to their problem. They took a number of small fish and put them in water, within a large glass bell jar that they then suspended into the water of the exhibit tank. Within minutes the large fish in the tank would take a run at the small fish, expecting to get a meal. Instead, what they got was a snout full of hard glass. They smashed their sensitive snouts against the sides of the glass jar and were denied their prize. Over time, the number of strikes by the large fish was eventually reduced to zero as the large fish in the aquarium came to learn that they could not eat the small fish. It became clear to them that their inability to eat these small fish was a condition of their life and that if they tried, it would only cause them discomfort. They learned to become helpless. After a period of time when no strikes were recorded by big fish on the glass jar, the aquarium handlers took the bell jar out of the exhibit and poured the small fish directly into the big tank. The problem was solved as the large fish continued to believe that they could not eat the small fish, and this belief was reflected in their behavior. Indeed, the large fish in the tank would starve themselves to death even though they were surrounded by a plentiful food supply. Their behavior is based on a false belief, but the consequence of that belief is as powerful as if the small fish were still protected by the walls of the glass bell jar.

How many times have you seen fundamentally flawed beliefs influence the thought processes and performances of individuals that you know? I certainly have seen the problem of learned help-lessness in the high-performance world in many occupations, whether we are talking about sport, business, or beyond. I am sure this problem causes billions of dollars in lost productivity world-wide each and every year. Our negative beliefs cause us to perceive the challenges that we face in work and life in a certain way, and that perception informs our health, our happiness, and, ultimately, our performance. We begin to believe that nothing we do matters and that fundamental belief influences everything!

Research suggests that we establish our personal belief system in early childhood, usually by the time we are eight years of age, or younger. Feedback that we receive from our parents and other important people in our lives serves as the first indicators of what we believe is our self-worth. As we grow older and develop, other "reflections" are held up to us by family members, friends, class-mates, teachers, coaches, and so on. This information tends to rein-force the feelings of worth or worthlessness that we learned at home, and these experiences form the basis of our self-image as we grow up and mature. By playing back images of inadequacy and failure, you program yourself to fail. Researchers have shown that the state of mental helplessness can even cause death.

 By consciously challenging such images and replac-ing them with pictures of competence and success, you can cancel your negative beliefs and replace them with positive ones that support your ability to perform with personal excellence. It all depends on the perspective you *choose* to adopt! Recognize that habits of thinking are not forever, we *can* learn to think about things in a different way.

The fear of failure is a primary reason most people do not set meaningful, challenging goals in the first place. They do not have the self-image to live with the possibility of failure. But you are never defeated until you accept defeat as a reality and decide to stop trying. The truth is, every failure is always a learning experience and it does not constitute failure unless you, a) give up, or b) fail to learn something that you can use in the future from the experience. Indeed, history shows how failure is essential to all achievement, that great success is almost always accompanied by failure. Thomas Edison had to discover more than 10,000 ways a lightbulb would not work before he discovered the one way that it would. He looked upon each unsuccessful experience not as a failure, but as a success because it taught him how the system would not work, and this perspective brought him one step closer to his ultimate goal. He was the most prolific inventor in modern history, with 1,097 devices patented in his name.

A Final Thought Concerning Perspective

I will admit that sometimes it is very difficult to find the silver lining when the cloud appears so dark and overpowering. How can you change your perspective on the challenging situation in front of you when you cannot think of a single positive thing about it? In this situation, you can always use my default thought process that goes something like this:

> *Well, that really sucks, and I cannot think of a single positive thing about this situation. But, it does yet again provide me with an opportunity to see what I am made of, to see if I have the backbone of a champion who can still bring the best he has to the situation, no matter how difficult that situation might be. It is an opportunity to measure myself against a significant challenge and see what kind of stuff I am made of.*

Simply choosing to look at the problem in this way now directs your thoughts and actions to focus on the task in front of you and to stop the mental digging that corrupts that task-focused mind-set. You can use the following simple protocol to help yourself to gain control over and effectively stop negative thoughts.

Rule #3 of the Mental Road states: "You can't *not* think about whatever is on your mind." In fact, the harder you try to not think about something that is negative, the more powerful and entrenched in your mind that negative thought becomes, and the greater the negative influence it has on your performance.

 The only way to stop negative thoughts is to *shift your thinking* to thoughts and images that are both positive and productive with regard to your personal performance.

Since the human mind can only process one thought at a time (Rule #2), you must actively choose to direct your mind toward (that is, focus on) a *dominant thought* that is positive, productive, and directly related to how you want to perform. By doing so, you will deny your mind the capacity required to dwell on the negative.

How to Stop Negative Thoughts

The **Five Rs** are key words that summarize a *negative-thought-stopping* procedure that can help you achieve this goal. Each word sets up the thought process for the next step in this sequential procedure. Implementing this thought process on a consistent basis, with deliberate thought and intent, is critical to successfully learning to stop negative or counterproductive thoughts. If you work at implementing this simple process, you will be surprised at how quickly it helps you to limit the occurrence of negative thoughts:

Recognize. Recognizing that you are having a negative thought is a critical first step in learning to control negative thoughts. Consciously increasing your awareness and vigilance with regard to negative thinking will aid in the recognition and control of counterproductive and self-destructive thinking. You must be *on guard* to recognize the *first signs* of negative thinking in order to crush that thought before it has a chance to fully form and strongly take hold of your conscious mind. You must become effective at eavesdropping on your own internal mind chatter and recognizing the earliest stages of negative thinking.

Refuse. You must refuse to allow the negative thought to continue and gain strength by some positive and defined action—for example, visualize a STOP sign in your mind's eye; snap a rubber band across your wrist every time you have a negative thought, and so on. You must do something to disrupt the negative image and/or thought in order to prevent it from growing stronger. By doing this, you begin the process of *shifting* your mind away from the negative thought.

Relax. Use any of a number of techniques that can help you to relax: take a deep, controlled breath; use a verbal trigger to shift your thoughts and feelings to a relaxing image, and so forth. When you are relaxed, the effect of mental programming is more powerful and you are ensuring that the next step in this five-step procedure will have an increased potential to be effective.

Reframe. The fourth step in the negative-thought-stopping procedure serves to complete the mind-shift toward images and thoughts that are consistent with your best performance. Replace the negative thought with a positive image or thought. "I *am* in control of my thoughts and actions, I can *choose* to respond and think the way I want to." "I've been here before and done this before, so I know I can do it again." "This is part of the process that I have chosen." Use imagery to "see" and "feel" the performance you want to achieve and how you want to *be* as you achieve it. *Become* your A.C.T. Model©.

Resume. Re-engage and continue your activities with a sense of confidence and control. You will always enjoy full confidence if you tie this to a personal commitment to always give your best effort, regardless of the situation or outcome. The degree of effort you apply to the challenges that you face on an ongoing basis is totally within your control. It is one of the few things that is, in fact, fully within your control. Think about what you are like when you perform with excellence and what you want to achieve, and grow your confidence by always applying your best effort to achieve it. A.C.T.© like a champion in word, thought, and deed.

Remember:

Your *perception* or *perspective* regarding the challenges you face will determine your emotional response.

Choose your perspective carefully, since the perspective you adopt is a choice that you make!

CHAPTER 11

RULE #7

If you do what you have always done, you will get what you have always gotten.
If you want something different, you must approach the challenges that you face with a different mind-set!

We are what we repeatedly do.
Excellence, therefore, is not an act but a habit.

—ARISTOTLE, PHILOSOPHER

If you successfully integrate the *Rules of the Mental Road©* into your day-to-day thinking, you will hold the secret to understanding how to program your mind for success. You will be better able to shape and control your dominant thought so that you can more easily slip into your mental zone of ideal performance, on command.

Since the mind can only process one thought at a time and because you can't *not* think about whatever is on your mind, your performance will be best served by implanting a dominant thought program in your mind that describes what you want and exactly how you will perform when you excel in the act of execution. If you focus on this mental program with intensity and single-mindedness, you will optimize your performance and will *never* suffer from performance anxiety. There will be no processor capacity available to process anything other than this positive and task-focused mind-set!

You should now understand more clearly how you sabotage yourself, and how the way that you think directly influences how you perform.

So, how do you change?

PART THREE

The A.C.T. Model© Process: Reprogramming Your Mind to Optimize Your Personal Performance

Introduction

Nothing contributes so much to tranquilize the mind as a steady purpose—a point on which the soul may fix its intellectual eye.

—MARY SHELLEY, NOVELIST, DRAMATIST, & BIOGRAPHER

The chains of habit are generally too small to be felt until they are too strong to be broken . . . how do you change a habit . . . only by replacing it with another habit.

—SAMUEL JOHNSON, AUTHOR, POET, ESSAYIST, & MORALIST

If you want to be a champion,
ACT the way a champion would act!

You may not recognize it as such but each of us is the product of a lifetime of mental conditioning. Whether it is the result of our educational experiences, our personal lives, our professional activities, or our recreational pursuits, we have been conditioned through our day-to-day experiences to exhibit behaviors that are consistent with the expectations we place on ourselves. These behaviors are invariably influenced and reinforced by feedback from our environment and from important individuals in our lives. While this conditioning is often positive and productive, it can at times also be negative and counterproductive.

When it comes time to "recondition" our mental programs, however, we must remember that the mind is different from a computer in that we cannot simply erase an old habit or mental program, like we can on a flash drive. We must *overwrite* the old program with a new, stronger one! Negative thinking patterns can be changed only by relearning different, more effective, and more productive thought patterns. To do so, we must become aware of what we want to change and then consciously repeat the new thought pattern we desire over and over again in our imagination, in order to imprint the new belief into our unconscious mind. We need to create a new performance *thinking* habit.

It stands to reason that if we sometimes program ourselves in a negative way, we can also turn this thinking around to begin to reprogram ourselves positively, to exhibit behaviors that are consistent with success at the highest levels. But how do we go about reconditioning ourselves mentally to consistently achieve this state of ideal performance, often referred to as *being in the zone*?

The goal of the A.C.T. Model© process is to create and implement a mental program that serves as an automatic pilot for *your* behavior. By creating a model of personal excellence that allows you to preset and reset your dominant thought, you will come to think and behave in a manner that is consistent with excellence within yourself. The A.C.T. Model© process uses the language of your mind (that is, it is based in imagery) and is designed to allow you to achieve a level of unconscious competence in those endeavors that you undertake. It is a systematic process that involves self-analysis and self-correction. It is a process that incorporates and integrates basic concepts drawn from six areas of science that speak powerfully to how our mind works: psycho-cybernetics, rational emotive therapy, control theory, autogenic training, neurolinguistic programming (NLP), and the principles of *learned helplessness* and *optimism*. It is not my intent here to discuss each of these approaches individually, but rather to reinforce the fact that the A.C.T. Model© process was not simply pulled out of thin air; there is a great deal of science that backstops the systematic approach utilized in this process. Those readers who are interested in this background information can read some of the excellent books and articles that have been written on these topics.

When my late partner and I designed the A.C.T. Model© process, we wanted to create a methodology that was simple, easy to implement (that is, doable), and effective. My experience working with thousands of high-performance athletes, occupational professionals, and business leaders over the decades affirms that the A.C.T. Model© process scores well on all three counts. Let us turn our attention now to the solution and answer the burning question:

"So How Do I Change?"

THE A.C.T. MODEL© PROCESS

The acronym used in the term A.C.T. Model© defines the three key steps that are used in this process of mental reconditioning. We will address each of these steps in turn in greater detail later in this last chapter. Here is what the process looks like, as an overview:

    A game   **C**ompare   **T**ransform

A—"A" Game

The "A" of the model identifies your personal standards of achievement, the standards that define *you* when you deliver "A" game performances. The first step in the process demands that you understand and identify the characteristics that underlie the mind-set you possess when you deliver your best performance—in a sense, your gold standards or standards of personal excellence. *You* must first define them. *You* must be able to see them, feel them, hear them, and so on. These standards become the achievement targets or goals associated with the mind-set you possess when you deliver your best performance, and once identified, the object of the process is ultimately to model them!

C—Compare

The "C" of the model describes the simple process of self-analysis that leads you to compare your actual performance with respect to each of your standards against your target or ideal standards. This establishes a gap between your current behavior or mind-set and the mind-set that qualifies as your "A"-game standard.

 By the simple act of establishing in your mind the gap between where you were and where you wanted to be, your unconscious mind automatically begins to reshape your emotions and behaviors in such a way as to move you toward those standards of personal excellence that are defined by the images in your mind and the feelings associated with them.

It is a standard gap-analysis methodology that sets up an automatic process of correction. Your unconscious mind takes its direction from your conscious dominant thought, and the "pendulum moves."

T—Transform

The "T" of the model guides you in the use of self-talk to input a clear, defined set of dominant thoughts and images that will fully influence your behavior and your performance in a positive way. With controlled positive and productive imagery and mind chatter, your own internal mental coach (that little voice in your head) will help to transform you into the performer that you want to be, and you will begin to exhibit to a greater extent the characteristics that are associated with excellence in *you*. Again, remember the influence of dominant thought on the movement of the pendulum.

While the establishment of a powerful and effective A.C.T. Model©
is best accomplished through an interactive, face-to-face process
with someone who understands how to extract the key descriptors
that connect at the deepest level for you, it is my intent here to walk
you through a series of steps that should allow you to create a personal A.C.T. Model©. This model will have the power to begin to
change your dominant thoughts and your behavior, and with better mental programs in place, the wrong mental programs will not
be processed (Rule #2). Let us now begin to develop your personal
A.C.T. Model©.

CHAPTER 12

STEP 1

Identify Your "A"-Game Standards

Seek out that particular mental attribute which makes you feel most deeply and vitally alive, along with which comes the inner voice which says, 'This is the real me,' and when you have found that attitude, follow it.

—WILLIAM JAMES, PSYCHOLOGIST, PHYSICIAN, & PHILOSOPHER

The first step in the A.C.T. Model© process demands that you identify the characteristics that define excellence in you, when *you* do your *best* work (these are *your* "A"-game standards). It is impossible for me to know what business, occupation, or sport you are engaged in, so out of necessity I will take a more generic approach to the process we will discuss in the coming pages. You will need to apply the process to your own situation.

Get comfortable, relax, and get ready to tap into your memory skills. As you go through this exercise, imagine that there is a magic camera trained on you, watching you closely and following your every move as you are engaged in the action of your performance, whatever it is that you are doing. It is a magic camera because, not only does it allow us to see what you look like from the outside as you perform, but it is capable of also looking inside you to understand what you are seeing in your mind's eye, and what you are feeling as you execute and engage in the task. Use this analogy of a magic camera as you study yourself to understand what character-istics define *you* when you do your best work. How do you think, feel, walk, talk, move, and so forth when you are on your "A" game? What would I see if I was watching you closely? What would the magic camera tell us about you by looking inside at your thoughts and feelings when you are at your best?

Now, I want you to direct this thought process to a specific event. Think back over the past to consider moments of best-ever performances, instances in your life where your personal perform-ance in your occupation or sport was as good as you can ever remember it being, when you were truly on your "A" game. Be clear in what I am asking here. I do not mean instances where the *result* you achieved at the end of that performance was the best ever, but rather that your personal performance while engaged in the task in front of you was superlative, absolutely the best you were capable of delivering!

Over the years, every one of my clients has reported that some of their best performances were not always associated with the best results they achieved, although there is usually a good correlation between moments of personal brilliance and positive outcome. Still, there were also times when performances that netted a lower finish-ing position still represented a better quality of personal perform-ance than other instances where these individuals finished at the top of the podium or "won." In this exercise, we are looking for the best personal performances you have ever achieved. Pick one that stands out in your mind when you were truly "in the zone" and recall your memories of that event. Reflect on this past best-ever experience (this exercise could take you thirty minutes or more), and consider the following questions as prompts to your memory:

- When and where did the performance you are thinking about occur?

- What time of the year was it?

- What was the weather like, if that is relevant?

- What time of day did the performance occur?

- Were there any unusual or unique circumstances concerning the event; anything important or out of the ordinary that stands out in your memory leading up to the event in question; or something that might have happened just before that competition or event to influence your mind-set at that time?

- Remember as best you can how the event unfolded—as you prepared for it and then as you stepped into the event ready to engage the task in front of you.

As you consider this best-ever experience, use the form presented in Table 2 and write in descriptive words or adjectives that reflect the set of mental images, thoughts, and feelings that exactly define what you are like, how you think, and who you are when you are mentally "in the zone." I do not want to put words in your mouth, but here are some examples of descriptors that could be used: aggressive, serene, deliberate, centered, smooth. Take the time to work through this brainstorming process carefully since it is the foundation that you will build upon to create your A.C.T. Model©. You are in effect creating a mind-map associated with your moments of personal brilliance, from a performance point of view. Please do not read any further before you complete this process.

Assuming that you have completed the exercise as I laid it out in the previous paragraph, take a moment to reflect on how you feel right now. As you thought back to this best-ever experience and sought to understand and put words to the mind-set, emotions, and feelings associated with that experience, did you begin to feel differently? If you engaged in the exercise properly, you could not help but begin to feel more like that individual who on the day of that performance delivered a moment of personal brilliance. It is likely that your mind-set shifted to become more aligned with the mind-set that exists when you performed to the best of your ability.

This is the power of dominant thought and the essence of the A.C.T. Model© process.

I asked you to complete this task before reading on because the descriptors or words that connect to the mind-set associated with championship performance *for you* must come *from you*. They must be your words. This is where the interactive process I mentioned previously can be very helpful in ferreting out the words that *truly* define that state of mind that possesses you when you perform to the best of your ability. Most often, the first words that are identified are not necessarily the right words, and an interactive process of discussion can help to find the most appropriate and powerful descriptors for each person.

In the absence of that process, however, I share with you (on page 190) those characteristics that many individuals identify as defining them when they are at their best. These are the descriptors they frequently use to describe the thoughts and feelings associated with their moments of personal brilliance.

TABLE 2: DESCRIPTORS THAT DEFINE ME WHEN I DO MY BEST WORK!

It has been clear from my experience that there are common threads or themes that the majority of people involved in the high-performance world share with respect to the state of mind that they possess when they do their best work. This observation is also supported in the research literature regarding flow state—the state of mind we possess when we are in the zone—and performance.

 My experience confirms that it does not matter what language high performers speak, how old they are, what culture they are from, what their gender is, or what their sport or job might be, the mind-set associated with excellence seems to be built from a surprisingly common platform.

In order to put structure to that platform, a number of years ago I examined the A.C.T. Models© of more than a thousand high-performance clients to extract and aggregate the descriptors that most commonly seemed to be reported by them as being associated with their moments of best-ever performance.

While not everyone identifies all of these basic behaviors as part of their personal model of excellence, and many individuals identify other variables that are not part of this common framework, there is enough of a consistency in these profiles for me to have pulled together eight common themes that seem to be associated with the mind-set that exists when people are "in the zone". These themes are not universal, but I suspect the frequency of their representation in the high-performance population would be astounding to most people, until you begin to understand the *Rules of the Mental Road*© and how they impact performance. I expect that many of the words, or at least the "intent" of those words, that you listed in Table 2 might ultimately be found in this common list. Let us now consider these common themes.

THE BASIC BEHAVIORS THAT UNDERLIE EXCELLENCE IN PERFORMANCE

Calm: Relaxed; Loose; Cool; Rested; At Peace; Detached; Unflappable; In Harmony; Comfortable; Composed; Free; Heavy; Breathe; Fulfilled; Serene; Tranquil; Chill; Secure; Grateful; Quiet; Blissful; Emotionless.

Focused: Here and Now; Single-Minded; In My Shell; Clearheaded; Centered; Sharp; Tuned In; Alert; In the Moment; Nonjudgmental; Fully Present; Locked In; Connected; Zeroed In; Clairvoyant; Issue at Hand; Alone; Head Up.

Confident: Arrogant; Bulletproof; Powerful; Strong; Walking Tall; Cocky; Dominant; Positive; Self-assured; Believe; Connected; Courageous; Bold; Well-prepared; Capable; Organized; Invincible; Committed; Superior; The MAN; Empowered; Puffed Out; Trust; Certain; No Doubt.

Energized: Pumped Up; Revved Up; Passionate; Joyful; Challenged; Enthusiastic; Fun; Excited; Motivated; Alive.

Intense: Tenacious; Persistent; Aggressive; Unstoppable; Hungry; On the Edge; Assertive; Predator; Purposeful; Relentless; Decisive; Panther; Lion; Shark; Dedicated; Determined; Fearless; Push the Limit; ALPHA.

Smooth: Rhythm; Fluid; Flow; Effortless; Easy; Nimble; Tempo; Slow Motion; Efficient.

Anticipatory: Analytical; Opportunistic; Adaptable; Smart; Adaptive; Flawless; Sensitive; Calculating; Open-minded; Flexible; Aware.

In Control: In Command; Measured; Patient; Professional; Responsible; Selfish; Precise; Methodical; Deliberate; Persuasive; Manipulate; Machiavellian; Chameleon; Inspiring; Balanced; Leader; Poised; Take Charge; Convincing; Accurate; Cunning;

Note that I have organized these sets of descriptors around a particular word that I have boldfaced and placed at the beginning of the grouping. There is *no* predominance of these words over any of the other words in the group; they are simply meant to encapsulate the underlying behavior or theme that is highlighted by the other words used in that specific category.

For example, some people prefer the word "calm" as a descriptor in their model, whereas others might prefer the words "serene" or "at peace" to convey the sense that there is an absence of "noise" in their head when they do their best work. The correct descriptor for each person is the word that connects them most powerfully to the images, feelings, and memories of what the state of mind represents for them when they are at the top of their game. Compare your words with this list. Are any of your words shared by others?

One of the striking things that stands out when we examine the list of descriptors above is that every one of these words speaks to an element of mind-set or behavior that is associated with execution, an in-the-moment oriented thought process. This is in sharp contrast to words that reference an outcome or a result such as coming in first, being the fastest, winning the race, or getting the gold medal.

It is indeed revealing that virtually all of these very successful high-performance competitors associate words that describe thought processes and emotions that relate directly to the quality of their execution (the "A" in our "A" x "B" = Results performance equation), rather than thoughts that represent a concern for or a focus on "B" factors, or even on "Results" when they perform to the best of their ability. This observation simply reinforces the fact that when we perform at our best, our focus of attention is necessarily directed toward the act of execution itself and not to the outcome that we hope or expect to see materialize. When they are in their "zone" of best performance, it appears that high-level competitors are indeed connected to what they are doing and fully engaged by the process of that execution. I would now like to take a few moments to briefly address the eight basic behaviors that seem to underlie the performance mind-set of many high level competitors:

Calm. This is a recurring theme that is highlighted in virtually every A.C.T. Model© I have reviewed in one form or another. If you think about it, this makes sense. It is very difficult for us to "hear" our inner voice talking to us and be guided by it to process the correct thoughts when our head is filled with "noise." When there is emotional upheaval, anxiety, and excessive mind chatter, it is really difficult to control and sustain our focus of attention on anything, for any length of time. A sense of mental or emotional calm is a necessary pre-/corequisite to the other underlying behaviors that appear to be part of our common framework for a high-performance mind-set.

Focused. If you think back to your best-ever performances, you will probably recognize that your focus was directed fully to the task in front of you and controlled by you, to attend only to execution-relevant information and decisions. It is not surprising to see that one of the descriptors used in virtually all A.C.T. Models© addresses what I described previously as the holy grail of the performance equation—the ability to focus in the moment on the task at hand, to the exclusion of all else. As you will recall, this was one of the two things (the other being about "confidence") that my clients routinely seek when they visit with me. It would be very difficult to explain why the word "focus," and by focus, I mean *correct focus* or *task focus*, would *not* be part of an individual's personal performance model.

Confident. The confidence that high-performance people talk about as being associated with their best work usually revolves around confidence in the knowledge and belief that they *can* be successful, not necessarily around confidence that they *will* be.

While many report that they "knew" that they would win, even in those situations their confidence seems to be more about the belief that they can handle whatever the situation throws at them and that they can overcome it. It is a supreme confidence in self. If we lack self-confidence and begin to doubt ourselves, our focus of attention naturally shifts to what it is that we are worried about, and we end up focusing on the wrong thing. The end result is that our personal performance is less effective than it could have been, regardless of the outcome that we achieve.

Energized. A sense of energy, enthusiasm, or excitement is often associated with the "A"-game performances of high-level competitors. This is where the aspect of "fun" lives and the passion that they feel for the occupation, activity, or sport that they are undertaking serves as emotional fuel that allows them to put in the ongoing effort required to be a top performer and a champion. It takes a great deal of energy to sustain our focus of attention for an extended period of time—that is, as we can all attest to, it is difficult to sustain a strong mental focus when we are physically fatigued—and the sense of energy that is associated with a championship mind-set supports our ability to focus effectively. Have you ever delivered an "A"-game performance when you felt sluggish or washed out?

Intense. The intensity that is associated with the typical A.C.T. Model© does not normally express itself as aggressiveness directed toward someone else. It is not about the competitor being angry or aggressive in the common sense of the word. Rather, it reflects an elevated level of intensity where the performer is "pushing the envelope" somewhat, and this state of mind can sometimes be interpreted by others as a level of aggressiveness. Often, clients talk about the need for patience so that they do not overreach, but follow that up with a recognition that they cannot be *too* patient or they will get left behind. The trick is to be *just patient enough* to operate within their control but push hard enough to make things happen as well. It does, however, set up a seemingly interesting contradiction.

The first descriptor we examined from the typical A.C.T. Model© was "calm," and yet here we identify the word "intense" as also being a common trait when we perform "in the zone." These two words seem to be in conflict with each other. How can we be both "calm" and "intense" at the same time? If you examine your thought process when you are in that zone of best performance, you will recognize that there is a blend of these two traits that can coexist nicely. It is indeed possible to be emotionally calm but physically and mentally intense at the same time, and when we are able to hit this "sweet spot," performing at a high level becomes somewhat effortless, even though we are potentially expending a great deal of energy.

What you must do is figure out what the blend of these two traits is that optimizes your performance, given what it is you do when you are in that moment of performance. Some activities might require a little higher level of intensity, usually when more physically powerful, gross motor tasks are involved; a lower level of intensity might be needed when the task involves fine motor skills and dexterity.

Of course, different people require different levels of "mental activation." Use the two gauges in Figure 19 to visually represent the level of activation that seems to optimize your performance. For reference, on the "calm" gauge, "0" means you are comatose, and "10K" represents the most wound up you have ever been in your life—that is, you are hitting your personal "rev limiter" and are maxed out! Calm does not even exist in your vocabulary when you are at this end of the scale. On the "intensity" gauge, "0" means that you are completely flat and totally passive, while "10K" on the scale represents a level of intensity that is as high as you are humanly capable of achieving. You are over the top! Where does your unconscious mind tell you that you should put your mark?

The identification of the specific level of these two traits really is an individual thing. Some people require a different level of psychological activation than do others, and neither is correct nor incorrect. The goal is for you to accurately identify the levels that optimize your performance so that the you can work on clearly defining the state of mind associated with these two characteristics and learn how to bring yourself to that level on command, using your personal A.C.T. Model©. It is important to understand the fundamental difference between being "tense," which is a bad thing generally, and "intense," which is often a good thing. If you can describe it and picture it with clarity in your own mind, you can model it!

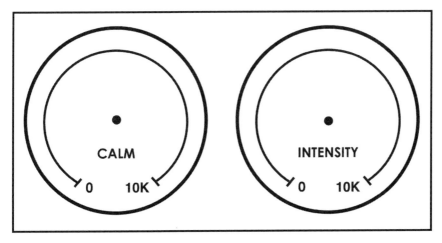

FIGURE 19. The relationship between "calm" and "intensity" when you do your *best* work.

I have discussed this juxtaposition of calm and intensity with my high-performance clients on many occasions and there is again a relatively narrow window that seems to be common to most of them when they perform at the highest level (illustrated in Figure 20). There is an optimal range that most speak about that is relatively consistently associated with the times in their competitive life when they deliver their best performances. Here is what they report:

On the "calm" side of the ledger, they speak about an optimal level at around 4,000 on the dial (where the range of responses might typically vary from 3,500 to 4,500 on our 10,000 point scale). It is clear that when they do their best work, there is indeed a sense of internal quiet that is evident (that is, an absence of mental "noise"), and this picture is consistent with the assertion that most people make that they do *not* generally perform at their best when they are anxious and preoccupied. Of course, we now know that one of the important reasons for this basic truth is that when we are anxious, our focus of attention shifts from what we should be focused on to what it is that we are worried about, and that incorrect focus directly affects our performance. How does your level compare to theirs when you are at your best? If you look at yourself with the eye of our magic camera, what does it see when you are in this place?

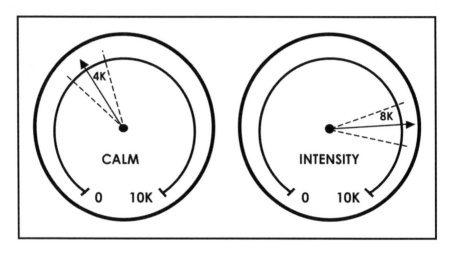

FIGURE 20. The relationship between "calm" and "intensity" for many in the high-performance world.

On the "intensity" side of the ledger, my clients often speak about an optimal level around 8,000 on the scale, where the range of responses typically varies from 7,500 to 8,500, depending on the person and the situation they are in. These numbers are simply a representation, a "gut" feeling if you will, as to the level of intensity that they operate at when they perform to the best of their ability.

It is again clear that their intensity, even in the most intense situations, is not at the top end of the scale. It is dialed back somewhat from the most extreme intensity that they are capable of. They report that if they are *too* intense, if they are pushing too hard or overdriving the situation, their performance suffers. What they are generally looking to find is that "sweet spot" where they feel somewhat emotionally calm but are capable of a high level of physical and mental intensity. This is not an easy place to find, but it helps to think about it in this way.

Unfortunately, what often happens (as illustrated in Figure 21), is that with the increasing worry that we sometimes feel, especially when we focus on results and the results are not what we had hoped that they would be, a calm mind-set slips through our fingers. The needle on the "calm" gauge starts to creep to the right. A natural response to this loss of calm and the increase in anxiety is that our "intensity" also begins an upward creep, and we end up overreaching or trying too hard. Our performance is usually never as good as it is when we work within that sweet spot.

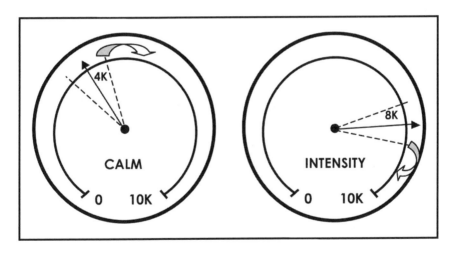

FIGURE 21. The relationship between "calm" and "intensity" when there is a loss of calm and an increase in anxiety.

Smooth. There is a sense of flow or rhythm to superlative performances. Whether I am speaking with a combat pilot, a race car driver, a golfer, a surgeon, a musician, or a sales professional, they describe a feeling of rhythm or tempo that helps to connect them intimately to the execution of the performance in which they are engaged. The more they can tap into this sense of rhythm, the better their focus on the task and the more they seem to be able to execute with smooth precision. Execution feels effortless.

Anticipatory. My clients speak about a sense of keen awareness that provides them with a mental reserve of processing capacity that allows them to adapt instantly to the evolving situation in their surrounding environment. Things sometimes seem to happen in slow motion. When they are "in the zone," they seem to be able to anticipate how the situation or performance will evolve, seemingly aware of what is going to happen even before it does. It is almost like they become somewhat clairvoyant.

In Control. When they are operating at their best, my clients talk about being in complete control of themselves, fully on top of every action they undertake. They are precise and accurate in their movements, deliberate in the way that they execute. Everything happens as they will it to happen. Even if they recognize that they cannot control other things, it almost seems as though they can. Their thought process seems to directly influence what happens around them. They are so connected to what is happening in the moment that they become the controlling agent in their environment.

Now that we have briefly overviewed the underlying behaviors that are frequently included in a personal A.C.T. Model©, it is time for you to take the list of descriptors you identified in the earlier exercise (in Table 2), and whittle it down into a list of the six to nine key variables that define who you are when you do your best work. There is no magic number to the A.C.T. Model© however. Some individuals feel that their model is more effective if they have a greater number of key words, while others feel that theirs is more effective when they have fewer. The downside of having too few descriptors in your model is that you might miss important underlying behaviors that could serve to connect you more powerfully to the state of mind associated with your best performances. The downside of having too many, on the other hand, is that the model becomes unwieldy and cumbersome. As such, the reflection you undertake when you consider those descriptors in your conscious mind becomes repetitious and blurs together because you have different words that are really speaking to the same quality or behavior. When you have too many words in your model, it also takes too long to fully implement the model, especially at the beginning. It must be simple and relatively easy to engage if the model is to be effective. It appears that for most people, a model that includes six to nine descriptors seems to work well.

The first step to begin to compress your set of personal descriptors into a functional A.C.T. Model© is to look at your list and identify the words that speak to the same quality, grouping them together along common themes. For example, if you have included the words "calm," "still," "quiet," and so forth, in your long list of words, these would likely fit within the same category. You can use a form with a structure similar to that of Table 3 to aggregate your words around common themes:

TABLE 3: GROUPED A.C.T. MODEL© DESCRIPTORS

Calm	Still
Serene	Quiet
Tranquil	At Peace
. . .	. . .
Intense	Revved Up
Predator	Aggressive
Unstoppable	. . .
. . .	. . .
. . .	. . .
. . .	. . .

Once you have extracted the common themes from the personal descriptors you previously identified from your past performance experiences, sit back and examine the groups carefully. Are there other qualities or behaviors that you missed in your list that would be important to include? Are there other words that could be included within each category that might be more effective and powerful at connecting you to the quality you are examining?

Once you are comfortable with your list of words that represent the key behaviors that you feel are associated with the mind-set *you* possess when you do your best work, the next step is to pick the one word from each category that you think is the most powerful for you. The word you select should be the one that connects you most strongly to the thoughts, memories, images, and feelings that define you when you are on your "A" game, *relative to that behavior.* Circle that word. You now have a key word or descriptor that identifies an important behavior or quality that you can associate clearly with thoughts and feelings that exist when you are in your zone of best performance. You may also have a list of second-level words that speak to the same quality or behavior but that are not quite as meaningful or powerful at connecting you to that behavior.

The A.C.T. Model© is not a checklist. It is not a set of words that you remind yourself of occasionally and do the mental equivalent of "checking the box." Rather, it is a process where the words of your A.C.T. Model© serve as portals to direct your dominant thought to reflect on the memories, images, and feelings associated with that descriptor when you are operating at the top of your game.

We can use the simple analogy of a room (as illustrated in Figure 22) to describe the process of what we are trying to accomplish. Imagine that we have a room with a door, on which a sign is affixed. The word painted onto the sign is the key descriptor for the behavior that you are seeking to model in your personal A.C.T. Model©. Let us assume for the purpose of discussion that the word on one of the doors is "calm." As we stand outside the room, we consider for a moment what "calm" represents for us when we are operating at the top of our game. As we step into this room (in our mind's eye), we observe different things. There are other signs on the wall that feature the words "serene" and "still." They give depth, texture, and color to the meaning of the word "calm." They help us to remember the nuances of what "calm" feels like when we are on our game. There are other things in the room as well. The square-looking shape might represent a clear memory of a past perform-ance experience where we were at the *perfect* level of calmness, a moment of performance excellence for us. The rounded-looking shapes might represent different illustrations that clarify "calm" in different ways: waves lapping quietly on the sea shore; a graphic equalizer from a stereo that moves from a series of wild gyrations to a low level of movement as our mind finds the perfect level of "calm" that optimizes our performance; the needle on the calm gauge being positioned at exactly the right spot, and so on. It is simply a process to guide your imagery, and ultimately, your

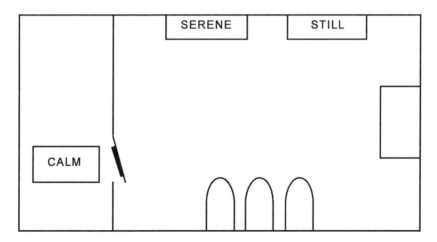

FIGURE 22. The A.C.T. Model© Imagery

dominant thought so that your unconscious mind can begin to move you in that direction and bring you to a state of emotional "calm" that supports your ability to perform with excellence.

Now that you have completed this refinement process, list your key descriptors in Table 4. Do not worry about the order of the words; we will tackle this task next.

The next step in developing your personal A.C.T. Model© is to establish the most effective progression of thought for the descriptors you have listed—that is, the order of the words in *your* model. While this part of the process gains much from the interactive process I mentioned previously, you will need to establish the order that you believe is most appropriate for you. Let me offer some food for thought that should help you in defining the most appropriate order. I will however come at it from what might seem like a strange direction.

Many years ago, there was a weekly television series that featured the adventures of Superman, a character that was born from an action comic. When Superman's alter ego, Clark Kent, received "the call" that someone was in distress and needed help, there was a series of actions set into motion that led him through a transformation process that took him from the persona of Clark Kent to that of Superman. If you saw this show, do you remember what started the process?

TABLE 4: MY PERSONAL A.C.T. MODEL©

The first thing that Clark Kent did was rip off his glasses with one hand and then immediately pull at his collar and tie to begin to loosen the knot as he darted off camera. We saw just a peek of the red suit that he wore underneath. Then the camera picked up Superman in his full costume as he bounded toward and out of a window or off a balcony, accompanied by the characteristic "whoosh" sound that came to represent his taking to flight. The transformation or metamorphosis of Clark Kent to Superman always happened the same way. There was a progression of action that was at the core of this transformation, and it started with him taking off his glasses in a certain way.

The transformation that is initiated by the A.C.T. Model© process is not unlike the metamorphosis of the fantasy character of Superman, except that instead of a progression of action involved in the transformation, it is a progression of thought. It sets into motion a new, systematic, and powerful dominant thought program that is directly connected to execution and to the mind-set that exists when we perform to the highest level of which we are capable.

We can illustrate this progression of thought by integrating the concept of the room I described previously with the idea of a suite of rooms connected by a long corridor. It would look like the illustration in Figure 23.

For the vast majority of the A.C.T. Models© I have guided individuals to develop over the years, there have been a couple of principles that seem to hold true for almost everyone. The first principle is that most of my clients select a descriptor that speaks to the issue of emotional calmness, the absence of mental noise, as the first element in their personal model. This occurs regardless of what the actual word might be that represents that state of mind for them, and regardless of the activity in which they are engaged. We first need to still the noise in our head so that we can properly hear our inner "little voice," and then direct our mind to process the right things. I believe that this same logic explains why most forms of the ancient martial arts, which involve high intensity, one-on-

one fighting, begin the process of combat with a period of meditation and relaxation to "quiet the spirit." This process also is common in many other sports and high-risk/high-demand occupations.

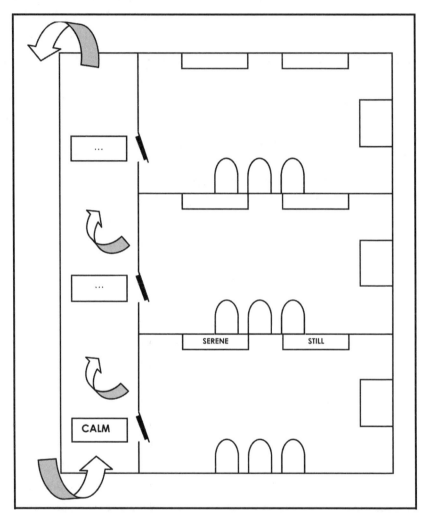

FIGURE 23. The A.C.T. Model© Imagery

The second principle to keep in mind when creating you A.C.T.
Model© is that the early part of the model tends to highlight behaviors that are more general in nature and speak to the mind-set that
is optimal in the competitive environment generally. Elements of

the model that come later tend to focus on behaviors that are quite specific to the process of execution that is employed in the moment of their actual performance. It is difficult to explain this progression in the abstract so I will use a sample of an actual person's A.C.T. Model© to help illustrate the point (see Table 5).

TABLE 5: A SAMPLE A.C.T. MODEL©

SERENE
CONFIDENT
PASSIONATE
INSPIRING
ENGAGED
MACHIAVELLIAN
FULLY PRESENT
PREDATOR

The model begins with the word "serene." It signals a quieting of mental noise and an adjustment of the "calm" dial to the optimal level for that individual and the performance in which he is engaged. This applies not only to the moment of performance but in the period leading up to and surrounding the actual perform-ance. It serves as an immunization (like a vaccine) against anxiety and worry.

"Confident" reflects the sense of belief-in-self that this individ-ual feels, recognizing that he has the knowledge, skill, and ability to get the job done. While he knows that he cannot control the out-come of his performance, he is confident that he can handle what-ever the competitive environment throws at him and likely prevail.

"Passionate" reflects the sense of enthusiasm and joy that he experiences when he is engaged in what he is doing. This passion that he has for what he does is the fuel that he uses to energize himself, to continue to persevere and put in the effort necessary to be a top performer. It reminds him that he is doing this because, fundamentally, he loves what he does. When it is not fulfilling and is not fun any longer, he generally does not do his best work. The first three elements of this individual's model speak to a set of important behaviors that preface his ability to be at the top of his game. It applies not just in the moment of the performance itself but in the window of time that surrounds that moment as well.

The word "inspiring" reflects the ability of this individual to lead, to effectively influence others to accept his point of view and come along for the ride. This descriptor begins to lean toward the actual performance, describing the individual's impact (from a distance) on others involved in the performance.

"Engaged" describes the sense of connection that the individual feels with respect to others involved in the performance, and to the task in which he is engaged. This individual does his best work when he is fully connected to the others around him and "all in" from a commitment point of view.

The term "Machiavellian" is often thought of as a negative one in that the common meaning associated with this term is that of a manipulator—something that is generally not thought of as being positive. For this individual, the term signals an expertise and an ability to effectively manipulate the individual(s) that he is involved with, but it is very much a positive term in that it speaks to his ability to control the flow of the performance and many aspects of the performance environment itself, to create a win-win situation for everyone.

The phrase "fully present" directs this individual to the specific task-focus that is the holy grail of the performance equation. Nothing else matters but what is happening in the moment of his performance. He is not partially present when he is on his "A" game; he is fully and completely here and now!

"Predator" rounds out this individual's model. This word, for him, aggregates all of the behaviors that are important to him into one metaphor: someone who is mentally and emotionally calm but capable of high levels of intensity when called for; patient enough, but supremely aggressive when it is required; intimately connected to the others in the environment, and in control of the situation around him; fully focused on what is happening in front of him as he waits for his prey and the exact, right moment to strike!

Of course this is an example of only one model but it serves to show a progression of thought that allows an individual to move from a state of internal quiet, where their mind is unencumbered by unimportant or disruptive information, to a mind-set where not only do they remain calm, but they are task-focused and capable of ruthless execution when necessary.

At this stage of the process, you should now have established the order of your initial A.C.T. Model© descriptors (transpose them into Table 6) and should be ready to begin to utilize your model of personal excellence to shape and reshape your dominant thought and your performance.

Now, on to the second step in the process!

TABLE 6: MY PERSONAL A.C.T. MODEL©

CHAPTER 13

STEP 2

Compare Your Behaviors and Thinking Relative to Your "A"-Game Standards

First say to yourself what you would be;
and then do what you have to do.

—EPICTETUS, GREEK PHILOSOPHER

The second step in the A.C.T. Model© process involves a regular and systematic self-analysis, particularly in the acquisition phase of the model. In essence, once you have established your personal "A"-game standards of excellence, you utilize these standards as a model to shape, in advance of your performance, and reshape, following your performance, your dominant thoughts associated with that performance.

The shaping part comes into play before you even engage your performance. In both *view mode* and *do mode*, imagine how you would perform when you execute with perfection. Imagine what you would look like and feel like as you successfully undertake the challenge in front of you. In other words, *use imagery to engage all of your standards of excellence,* and let those standards possess you! By thinking about the qualities that define excellence in you, by using your A.C.T. Model© as a conscious-mind framework, you automatically establish the correct dominant mental program that ultimately guides your unconscious mind to shift your thinking to be consistent with that mind-set. The pendulum moves. It really is that simple, even though it requires discipline to purposefully and deliberately engage the process.

The reshaping part comes into play after the performance has been completed and it is time to evaluate how well you did. You compare the behaviors and mind-set that defined you during the performance you just completed versus your personal model of excellence. You answer the simple question: "How did I do, relative to my "A"-game standards"?

For each standard in your personal model of excellence, identify and imagine your desired standard as it would have been delivered in that performance you just completed. Establish the "gap" in your mind. See and feel the *difference* between what you achieved (that is, how you executed/performed), and how you wanted to feel and think while you achieved it for each of your standards during that performance. You can create a log book or journal to give structure to this systematic self-analysis process and use a form like that shown in Figure 24 to complete that evaluation. Put a *single* mark across the line based on your subjective feeling, to establish the quality of your actual performance versus your ideal performance standard for that behavior (I have placed *two* marks on the line, but I will explain why in a moment).

FIGURE 24: A.C.T. MODEL© STANDARDS OF EXCELLENCE *(Example)*

POOR ————————————————— IDEAL

_____ CALM _____

1 — 2 — 3 — 4 — 5 — 6▌— 7 —▌8 — 9

_____ . . . . _____

1 — 2 — 3 — 4 — 5 — 6 — 7 — 8 — 9

My Personal Performance

1 — 2 — 3 — 4 — 5 — 6 — 7 — 8 — 9

You will note that in Figure 24, the line for each A.C.T. Model© descriptor is anchored by the numbers "1" (poor) and "9" (ideal). A "1" on the scale means that the quality of your performance was the *worst* you have *ever* been while a "9" on the scale means the *best* you have *ever* been—exactly where you wanted to be! Realize that a "9" does *not* mean the *most* you have *ever* been. We can use the first descriptor—"calm"—to clarify this point further. In some performance situations, you do not want to be as calm as you have ever been because being too calm may cause you to be too lethargic (remember, the ideal level on our "calm" dial is around 4,000, not 0 or even 1,000, for most individuals), and that would not optimize your performance. A "9" on this scale would indicate that the performance unfolded at *exactly the right level* of calmness for the situation. If you are either too high or too low on the "calm" dial, it is *not* "ideal" and therefore would not be scored as a "9."

In the abbreviated form in Figure 24, I placed two marks across the line in order to give you a sense of reference. One of the marks is just short of the "8" on the scale, while the other is just right of the "6" on the scale. It is clear that both marks establish a gap between their position and the "9" on our scale, but it is obvious that placing the mark near the "8" means that you were much closer to the ideal level of calmness for the situation than you would have been if you had placed your mark near the "6." There is not much of a shift required in your internal level of calmness to move yourself into that sweet spot referenced earlier when you are close to "8" versus when you are near the "6." The difference between where you were and where you wanted to be is smaller.

You will also note that at the bottom of Figure 24, there is a statement that reads: "My Personal Performance." Use the same type of gap analysis to evaluate and highlight the strength of your overall performance. This is not a reflection of how successful you were in achieving your goal (in the meeting or the negotiation, for example), or how well you placed in the competition, or how high your finishing position was, but rather, it is intended to reflect the overall *quality* of the performance you delivered, in comparison to that which you would have delivered had you truly been on your "A" game. I have included an example of what the full form might look like (Figure 25), for your reference.

Figure 26 (on page 214), sharing a similar layout, is designed to pull together a number of general behaviors that are common to individuals who perform at a high level and that are important for all of us to master. Some of the elements listed in this form may not always apply since the situation you are evaluating might not lend itself to including them. If this is the case, simply leave them blank and pick only those elements that are relevant to the performance you are actually evaluating, or change them to suit your needs.

Keep in mind that what we are discussing here is a process, and as such, it can apply to any action or performance you undertake in any aspect of your life. By adopting this type of process—either formally with a logbook using forms like those described here, or informally, just undertaking the analysis in your own mind—this approach can help you to perform that task at a higher level. You just have to determine what the standards of excellence are *for you* performing that task and then use the A.C.T. Model© process to help you clarify and implement what you need to change within yourself to execute more effectively.

Since your unconscious mind takes its direction from your conscious mind, you are effectively reprogramming your mind by using performance-based imagery of the thoughts and feelings associated with you when you do your *best* work. The "compare" step of the A.C.T. Model© process requires that you execute a simple gap analysis in answer to the question: "How did I do in that performance situation?" Placing a mark across the line for each of the descriptors in your personal model of excellence establishes that gap in performance and sets up the next and final step of the process.

FIGURE 25: PERSONAL A.C.T. MODEL©
STANDARDS OF EXCELLENCE

POOR ——————————————————— **IDEAL**

1 — 2 — 3 — 4 — 5 — 6 — 7 — 8 — 9

1 — 2 — 3 — 4 — 5 — 6 — 7 — 8 — 9

1 — 2 — 3 — 4 — 5 — 6 — 7 — 8 — 9

1 — 2 — 3 — 4 — 5 — 6 — 7 — 8 — 9

1 — 2 — 3 — 4 — 5 — 6 — 7 — 8 — 9

1 — 2 — 3 — 4 — 5 — 6 — 7 — 8 — 9

1 — 2 — 3 — 4 — 5 — 6 — 7 — 8 — 9

1 — 2 — 3 — 4 — 5 — 6 — 7 — 8 — 9

My Personal Performance

1 — 2 — 3 — 4 — 5 — 6 — 7 — 8 — 9

FIGURE 26: GENERAL BEHAVIORS

POOR ——————————————————— IDEAL

General Mood Control

1 — 2 — 3 — 4 — 5 — 6 — 7 — 8 — 9

Physical Stress Control

1 — 2 — 3 — 4 — 5 — 6 — 7 — 8 — 9

Mental Stress Control

1 — 2 — 3 — 4 — 5 — 6 — 7 — 8 — 9

Anger Control

1 — 2 — 3 — 4 — 5 — 6 — 7 — 8 — 9

Nutritional Discipline

1 — 2 — 3 — 4 — 5 — 6 — 7 — 8 — 9

Communication

1 — 2 — 3 — 4 — 5 — 6 — 7 — 8 — 9

Organization

1 — 2 — 3 — 4 — 5 — 6 — 7 — 8 — 9

Problem-Solving Ability

1 — 2 — 3 — 4 — 5 — 6 — 7 — 8 — 9

_____

1 — 2 — 3 — 4 — 5 — 6 — 7 — 8 — 9

CHAPTER 14

STEP 3

Use Self-Talk (Your Own Internal Coach) to Transform Yourself and Reprogram Your Unconscious Mind!

It is the habitual thought that frames itself into our life.
It affects us even more than our intimate social relations do.
Our confidential friends have not so much to do in shaping
our lives as the thoughts which we harbor.

—J.W. TEAL, PSYCHOLOGIST & BUSINESS LEADER

The final step in the A.C.T. Model© process involves *talking to yourself,* using that little voice in your head (your own internal coach) to transform yourself to become just like the standard of excellence in your model. You accomplish this by answering the questions: "How would I have been different if I had been 'excellent' in that performance situation?" "What would have been different *about me* if I had been at the very top of my game, for each descriptor in my personal model of excellence?"

To answer these questions, use imagery associated with your personal standards of excellence and use self-talk to clearly see and feel *what* and *how* you would change to embody the ideal standard for each word in your model. Review the situations that occurred over the period you are evaluating and *transform* yourself, using imagery, to respond to those same situations in the way that you would like to have responded. In your mind's eye (understanding the difference in "feel" that is associated with such a shift), move from your actual level of performance (as you perceived it to be) to your ideal level of performance for each of the descriptors in your A.C.T. Model©. Imagine yourself *transforming* from where you were to where you want to be. See the metamorphosis involved and imagine what it would feel like. The challenge is to *become* your *model of excellence* on a consistent basis and "live it" in everything that you do!

For some individuals, it is very helpful (especially in the early implementation stage of the A.C.T. Model©) to build a journal component into their personal logbook. I have built such a component into the logbook that I designed for my clients for many years, and while this type of tool does not suit everyone's style, it has been adopted, adapted, and used by many. I include two self-feedback forms that have a structure as outlined in Figures 27 and 28:

FIGURE 27: PROBLEM BOX
(where I summarize the problems . . .*briefly*)

(This form should be *no bigger* than this!)

FIGURE 28: SOLUTIONS BOX
(where I write about solutions; about how I want to be)

(This form should be *much bigger* than this!)

With respect to the Problem Box shown in Figure 27, it is important to keep the space small. The goal of delimiting the size of this area is to force the individual to encapsulate or summarize the main problem(s) briefly, not to spend a lot of time elaborating the details of the problem. It could be a commentary such as: "I did not do a very good job today at staying focused on the task. I kept letting my mind wander to worry about whether or not I would be successful." The reason for this decision is simple—Rule #3 of the Mental Road© informs us that we "Can't *not* think about whatever is on our mind!" The more space we allocate to expand on the negative points that relate to our performance, the more size, weight, color, and structure we give those negative thoughts, entrenching them into our unconscious mind. This is not an "ostrich with our head in the sand" technique; it is important to identify the problem areas we encounter. However, it is sufficient to boil the problem down to its core issues to understand what needs to be changed, and how to begin to make that shift.

As far as the Solutions Box is concerned (Figure 28), take all the pace you want! This is where you would write "notes to self" concerning the correct mind-set associated with your ability to perform at an "A"-game level during the performance you are evaluating. It could be a narrative; it could be bullet point notes—it does not matter how you put your thoughts down but rather that you get them down. Writing them down forces you to consolidate your thoughts concerning the performance you are self-evaluating, with a view to describing the look and the feel, as well as the actions that you would have taken had you performed with excellence. Writing them down also forces you to really focus on what you are doing. Some clients prefer to create entries associated with each of their A.C.T. Model© descriptors, while others prefer an overall narrative. There is no correct or incorrect way to accomplish this final step of the process.

By way of example, to describe what kind of information might go into this Solutions Box, I would like to share with you some actual journal entries of one of my high-performance clients who visited with me because he was struggling to put together performances at a level that he had previously delivered with ease. I include this example here only to illustrate how Joe's (this is not his real name) thinking and focus shifted to a more execution-focused mind-set as a result of actively engaging his A.T.C. Model©, and his logbook entries articulated this change quite well. First, I will tell you a little about Joe.

Joe was a front-tire changer for one of the top NASCAR Cup race teams competing on the circuit in that year. He was recognized by many of his peers as being one of the top changers in the business, but of late he had been struggling to deliver the kind of pit stop performance that was essential at this level of competition. The more errors he made, the more he worried about making errors and being slow, and of course, the more he then made errors and was indeed slow. As time went on, he worried excessively and ended up focusing on the wrong thing. The problem was becoming more serious as he was costing his team as much as 1.5 to 2.0 seconds per stop, a huge problem in their world! The team did not want to let him go, however, because they knew what kind of performance he was capable of, so they asked me to spend some time with him. Together, we developed his A.C.T. Model© and he set to work implementing the process into his racing and his life.

Three of the eight descriptors in Joe's model were: "loose," "crisp," and "in control." If you think about what a tire changer must accomplish during a pit stop in a race situation, these descriptors make sense. The journal entries below are taken verbatim from his personal logbook, purely for the purpose of illustration, from three separate time windows:

- **Time 1 (T1):** The week after his visit with me when he really just started working with his personal A.C.T. Model© (this coincided with the following weekend race on the competitive calendar).

- **Time 2 (T2):** Two weeks following Time 1, again at a subsequent race event on the calendar.

- **Time 3 (T3):** Two weeks following Time 2, at another race.

LOOSE

- T1—"Still a little tense from the week before. I would have been a lot better if I didn't have to prove I could do it. A "9" would have been mellow, not so much weight on my shoulders."

- T2—"The 'loose' feeling was great, the best I've felt in months. Man I love that feeling, *no* tension. It felt like the weight was lifted off my shoulders."

- T3—"Lighter than anything you could imagine. *No* worries, tension, or nervousness. Limber like a piece of thread. Walking tall, head high, shoulders back, feeling really good. Just another walk in the park. Jumping perfectly, landing perfectly, every movement felt looser than ever."

CRISP

- T1—"Movements, sight were okay but not up to par. Hand and eye coordination would have been better, more precise. Jabs and pulls would have had less mistakes."

- T2—"Sharp, quick movements felt snappy . . . it felt good. It was like hitting, moving, like you never did before with fun and excitement. It was next to perfect, the way it's supposed to be. The old but new (Joe) is back!"

- T3—"Running to the car, every stride felt solid. Going down on one knee, then the other, was firm and precise. Hitting lugs harder than ever, like I was a hydraulic ram. Not rough but sharp, hard, fast jabs. Very stable movements . . . short, sweet, hard, and right on target."

And finally, IN CONTROL

- T1—"I felt better in control than last week. Need more work in that area. It would have been awesome if I would stop, slow down, and do it. A '9' would have been a mistake-free day."

- T2—"I was so focused it felt like nothing could go wrong. I felt every movement. The accuracy, the timing of the jump, kneeling down to start, hitting nuts—I was on top of the world . . . unstoppable."

- T3—"So fast, accurate. Movements were precise and on time. I could see a little more detail than usual. So focused the movements felt automatic and natural. I didn't feel rushed or pressured, I was energized. Jumping, running, kneeling, hitting nuts, pulling tires . . . I felt like no energy was used."

Interesting progression of thoughts over the period of a month, is it not? Needless to say, as Joe figured out in a very short period of time how to control his focus of attention to be on the right things at the right time, and was able to direct his thoughts to the specific behaviors and actions that made him the top performer that he was, his performance came back to him. It is indeed funny how that works!

The holy grail of the performance equation is the ability to focus on the task in front of you, to the exclusion of everything else in that moment that simply serves to distract you from that performance imperative. If you develop the ability to control and sustain that type of focus, you will deliver the best performances you are capable of. It is unreasonable to expect more than that from anyone.

Now, before I bring this final chapter of the book to a close, I would like to briefly address the concept of "anchors" and "triggers."

Anchors and Triggers

Your personal A.C.T. Model© is a set of descriptors or achievement standards (the "A" of the A.C.T. Model©) that define the state of mind that is consistent with excellence in performance . . . for you. The qualities and behaviors identified within your model are reflected by words that are meant to powerfully invoke the images and feelings associated with those qualities—qualities that show through strongly during your best-ever performances.

In a very real sense, the A.C.T. Model© is a personal model of excellence that defines your "A" game—how *you* think, feel, and behave when you perform at the highest level that *you* are capable of. Strive to produce clear, vivid, and animated images associated with each of the achievement standards in your model. Do not just visualize each standard of excellence, you must also "feel" the behaviors associated with your best-ever performances. The more you can include the different senses in your mental imagery of excellence, the more powerful will be the positive effect of this mental reprogramming on your ability to perform with excellence.

An "anchor" is usually a physical action that becomes associated with a set of feelings and images, through the process of repetition. For example, you may have noticed that some people physically shrug their shoulders when they do not know the answer to a question they might have been asked, or snap their fingers when they recall something that they were supposed to remember. We have developed many anchors in our life. Some produce good feelings and others may be associated with feelings of apprehension and insecurity (such as "wringing" of the hands when under the influence of negative stress). The A.C.T. Model© process seeks to anchor a physical action to the positive and productive mind-set that exists in your personal zone of excellence. The process is straightforward: if you first anchor a physical action to the mind-set that exists when you are in your zone of best performance through quality repetition, you can then use the same physical action to "trigger" this mind-set—to bring about the feelings and images associated with your personal model of excellence.

Your anchor can be any simple physical action you choose (for example, making a fist with your hand, snapping your fingers, a special way to take a breath, touching the knuckles of one hand, and so forth). When the images and feelings associated with all of the achievement standards that make up your A.C.T. Model© are fully realized *in your imagination,* carry out the physical anchor at the peak of your mind-body experience and mentally "tie" this feeling to the physical anchor you just executed. Do this twice a day over four consecutive days to *set the anchor*. Then, over the period of twenty-eight days, continue to vividly and with conviction imagine the standards of excellence in your A.C.T. Model© on a daily basis. Ensure that you continue to tie your physical anchor to this mind-set of excellence, and once you have completed this process over twenty-eight consecutive days, you will have created a habitual way of thinking that is consistent with your *best* performance.

Once your physical anchor is strongly associated with this mind-set of excellence, the anchor can be used to trigger this mind-set as you engage your performance, and on command. In this way, the execution of your physical anchor can serve to activate your performance-ready mind-set and your mental program of excellence will be set in motion no matter how many distractions you face or how difficult the situation might be. Your unconscious mind will take its direction from your conscious mind, triggered by the action you have tied to the feelings involved in that mind-set of excellence.

Conclusion

There you have it! The A.C.T. Model© is a simple, methodical process of self-analysis and self-correction. However, it is *not* a magic bullet. It requires a deliberate, purposeful, and consistent implementation of dominant thought control to change your thinking and your performance. If you apply this process to your work and to your life in general, you will become better at getting out of your own way. Your unconscious mind will take its direction from a new set of powerful, positive, and task-focused dominant thoughts, and this mind-set will optimize your personal performance. It will also increase the likelihood that you will accomplish the performance goals you set for yourself. It does not guarantee outcomes, of course, but it does provide for a better chance of achieving them.

How will you know that your A.C.T. Model© is working? How does it express itself in the things that you do? There are as many different applications of this performance-modeling process as there are individuals and situations that they find themselves in. Let me offer an example that may help you to understand how the process can be integrated into the tasks that you might undertake, and how it might change your actual performance, as well as the potential outcome.

Let us imagine that you are getting ready to head into an

important meeting where you must present your analysis of a complex situation and outline specific recommendations for action. If you are successful at making your case, the company will move in a particular direction, and if not, it may head in a different direction. There is a lot of money at stake and it is a pressure-filled situation because there are competing solutions being considered.

For some individuals thrust into this type of situation, their overriding response as they step into the meeting room is one of worry. You may dwell on the fact that if you are unsuccessful in convincing the company's executive team about the benefits of your solution over that of other strategies being considered, the company may make a mistake as far as you are concerned, and lose a lot of money. In addition, you may worry that failure to make your case might undermine the confidence that you believe senior management has had in your decision-making ability in the past. Perhaps you beat yourself up over prior mistakes and the less-than-ideal results that you may have accomplished in similar situations in the past, and fear that a similar outcome may come to pass this time as well. This fear of failure becomes dominant in your conscious mind, and this focus causes your anxiety to increase. You risk tunnel vision as you lose the mental flexibility to think on your feet. If you perceive that things are not going well as the presentation unfolds and that your fears are being realized, you end up focusing less on the connection you are making with your audience and more on thoughts that you are not getting the job done. Failure threatens even more to become a self-fulfilling prophecy.

With an A.C.T. Model© in place, however, the situation could be quite different. The meeting is just as important and the situation offers just as much pressure as it did before, but your personal response to it is different. As you begin to engage your personal model of excellence in advance of the meeting, you remind yourself that you cannot control the outcome of the meeting. You also take the time to recognize that the outcome you are working toward has a greater chance of being realized if you remain calm, confident in your own abilities, and task-focused. As you prepare for your meeting, you recall past experiences and gradually come to adopt the same mind-set that you possessed when you excelled in similar situations in the past. As you step through the descriptors of your personal A.C.T. Model© in your conscious mind— descriptors that define who you are and how you think when you are at the top of your game—your unconscious mind responds and takes you to that place. You enter the meeting room with a more task-focused and calm mind-set and since this mind-set persists as you engage your performance, your mind does not become preoccupied by negative thoughts associated with anxiety and failure. You are more likely to connect with your audience and clearly outline your ideas and plan in the most effective way possible. Because you are more relaxed and tuned-in to the issues and concerns that are of specific interest to individual executive team members, you respond more effectively to any questions that are raised. All things being equal, what situation do you believe is likely to yield the best result?

Each of us has the choice to think and act either positively or negatively, constructively or destructively. If so, why on earth would anyone choose to think negatively? The point is that no one *consciously* makes a choice each time we think. Our unconscious mind predisposes us to one type of thinking or another, based upon our personal mental programming, which in turn is based upon our overriding dominant thought.

Old thought patterns *can* be replaced with new, more productive mental programs; it just takes the will to do so and the consistent work necessary to achieve it. It involves increasing your level of awareness of what you want to change and consciously repeating the new learning experience you desire over and over again in your imagination.

The majority of high-performance people would agree that 80 percent of the game is mental. It does not matter whether we are talking about a touring golf pro, a company CEO, a SWAT team specialist, a top salesman, a racing driver, a surgeon, or a successful financial trader. They recognize that it is not their physical prowess or their knowledge that ensures success in the competitive world in which they live and work. Rather, they realize that their personal success is most influenced by the mental skills that they are able to bring to bear on the tasks that they undertake on a day-to-day basis, and at the very moment of the major events in their lives.

Even though mental skills are acknowledged as being a critically important part of the performance equation, most of us invest little time and effort in working on this aspect of our personal performance. Part of the reason stems from the trait characteristic that we human beings possess that causes us to look for the easy way to do just about everything. The marketplace is filled with very financially successful products that promise the "quick fix," the modern-day equivalent of the "magic pill." But developing mental skills is not unlike developing your physical fitness. It takes time, effort, and dedication to develop the kind of mental toughness that high-performance people work diligently to develop.

As you improve your mental skills, you will learn to associate the images and feelings of what you are like (what it "feels" like) when you are appropriately focused and on task. Once you are aware of these images and feelings, you will be able to effectively apply this improved control over your focus of attention to other complex tasks you might undertake.

 You must provide your unconscious mind with a new goal-image if you want to bring about change; otherwise, it will automatically refer back to previous programming for its instructions. You always act the part, unconsciously, of the person you see yourself to be. It is important to choose wisely!

With quality practice, you will understand how to control and direct your focus so that it is appropriate to the demands of any activity in which you are involved. If you successfully integrate the seven key *Rules of the Mental Road©* into your day-to-day thinking (and maintain that mind-set—this is the key), you will possess the secret of how to program your mind for success. You will understand how to powerfully shape your dominant thought so that you can more easily slip into your mental zone of peak performance, on command. Remember that your mind can only actively process one thought at a time (Rule #2) and the truth is that you can't *not* think about whatever is on your mind (Rule #3). Your performance will be best served by implanting a dominant program in your mind that describes exactly what you want and how you want to be when you perform with personal excellence, *in the moment.* If you focus on this mental program, you will find it easier to maintain the relaxed and confident frame of mind that is consistent with your best personal performance.

The focus of this book has been to help you to better understand and improve your *individual* personal performance. In the end, this is the only thing over which you have complete control. The next step in your quest to maximize your results is to understand how you fit within your team's or group's environment. Besides the need for you to bring your "A" game to your performances individually, your interaction with other members of a team can and does have an influence on the overall team's success. Issues related to communication, trust, and team culture become critically important to the organization's process and methodology to create success, and you must give these important aspects of team effectiveness some thought. While these topics were beyond the scope of the present work, recognize that the basic *Rules of the Mental Road©* apply here as well, and that the A.C.T. Model© process can be adapted to serve the needs of organizations.

What can you control? You can control your thinking, if you take the time to become aware of it and take command of it. You can control the things that you choose to believe in and the way you see yourself. You can control what you imagine and the direction in which you want your future to unfold. You can control the goals you set for yourself and the way you go about achieving them. You can control the things that you eat and the exercise that you engage in. You can control who you associate with and the topics of conversation that you are willing to engage in. You can control the environment you learn and live in, and the people, places, and things that influence your thinking and behavior. You can control *your response* to every situation and circumstance in your life.

It is a fact that *the human mind does not distinguish between what is real and what is vividly imagined!* This basic truth (and process) applies to every single role and aspect of your life. It is not just about your work or competitive environment; these principles are fundamental, universal, and infallible!

As I bring this book to a close, I want to share with you the story of one of my clients, a friend who you may have heard about, because of his successful exploits on a couple of fronts. His name is Helio Castroneves, a world-class race car driver who currently competes in the IZOD Indycar Series for the iconic Team Penske organization. As a young boy, Helio was so passionate about racing as a career-professional that he travelled with his family from his home in Sao Paulo at the age of 15 and flew to Italy to compete in the karting World Cup, one of the most significant international karting events of the year. In his first big international race in unfamiliar equipment, he finished a credible 16th out of 150 drivers. His racing career on the world stage was launched.

I started working with Helio in 1996 when he first came to the United States to drive for Steve Horne's Tasman Motorsport team in the Indy Lights Series. He visited with me and my late partner, Dan Marisi, in Daytona Beach, Florida, at the request of his team owner, because he was struggling with uncertainty and self-doubt. In spite of his proven talent, he was sabotaging himself, and his performance was suffering. He could not figure out how to stop it. We spent time with Helio as he went through the steps of our comprehensive performance program, and he learned a lot of things about himself. He came away from the experience with a much clearer understanding as to exactly how he sabotaged his own performance, and the A.C.T. Model© process that he left with became the foundation of his mental approach to competition and to his own performance.

Over the years, together we have adapted Helio's A.C.T. Model©. He continues to rely on it to this day to establish and sustain the mind-set of the champion he has proven to be. He has won numerous races in Indy-style racing cars since he first competed in the series in 1998, but his biggest accomplishment to this point is winning back-to-back Indy 500 race events in 2001 and 2002, and then following that up with yet a third win at the hallowed track in 2009—the only Brazilian driver to ever do so and only the sixth driver in the history of this prestigious event to have accomplished this task. By his own admission, the A.C.T. Model© process has sustained him well in his racing career thus far. Its impact however, has extended beyond racing for Helio.

In 2007, because of his success on the race track and his personality, he was invited to be a contestant on ABC's wildly popular *Dancing with the Stars* television program. Helio would be the first person to tell you that he really is not a dancer, that he is no better at the art of ballroom dancing than the average person might be! While he can drive a race car, he will tell anyone who listens that he really is not very good at moving his feet to the beat of the music. But true to form, once committed, Helio engaged the task with the same level of professionalism and gusto that he approaches all the challenges that he tackles. He and his dance partner, Julianne Hough, practiced their routines tirelessly and he simply did as he was told. Julianne coached him on what specifically he had to do, and he executed her wishes to the best of his ability. He shared with me how he had adapted his A.C.T. Model© to this new role as a dancer and reflected on the likelihood that he would never have been able to accomplish what he did without this process that helped him to bring the task-focused, championship mind-set to the dance floor that he needed every day. In November of 2007, Helio and Julianne were crowned Season Five *Dancing with the Stars* champions, and he proudly displays his hard-won mirror-ball trophy in his home.

The purpose behind sharing this story with you is to simply reiterate that the A.C.T. Model© is *a process* that *anyone* can use to help themselves to perform to the highest level that they are capable of. Helio can certainly drive a race car and he has a genuine talent to do it well. But he applied the same mental control process that he had *learned* and has used successfully in racing to something that was quite foreign to him. Yet, with hard work and some athleticism, he was able to adapt this process and use it to achieve a goal he set for himself in a highly competitive activity that was very much outside of his comfort zone. He would argue that if he can do it, anyone can.

A short time ago, one of my other high-performance clients sent me an e-mail in which he stated:

> "On a personal note, I have found that if I work my model frequently and stay with it, I almost don't notice that it exists and is helping me (it is taken for granted). If I don't stay on a little maintenance, it takes more effort and I certainly notice that I don't have it helping me. It is a state of mind that you almost don't even notice when you have it, but sure notice when you don't."

I couldn't have summarized it better myself . . .

I encourage you to stay in control of your focus of attention and strive to simply deliver the best you are capable of every time you are called upon to perform . . . win, lose, or draw!

—JACQUES DALLAIRE, PH.D.

Recommended Reading

Learned Helplessness: A Theory for the Age of Personal Control, by Christopher Peterson, Ph.D., Steven F. Maier, Ph.D., and Martin E. P. Seigman, Ph.D. Oxford University Press (1995).

Learned Optimism: How to Change Your Mind and Your Life, by Martin E. P. Seligman, Ph.D. Vintage Books, a division of Random House, Inc. (2006).

Psycho-Cybernetics, by Maxwell Maltz, M.D. Prentice-Hall, Inc. (1960).

Psycho-Cybernetics 2000, by Maxwell Maltz Foundation and Bobbe Sommer, Ph.D. Prentice-Hall, Inc. (1996).

Index

About the Author

Dr. Jacques Dallaire received his doctorate in exercise physiology from the University of Alberta (Canada) in 1979. He taught at McGill University in Montreal for five years before assuming the then newly created position of Manager of Science and Medicine Programs at Sport Canada (a division of the Canadian government's Ministry of Fitness and Amateur Sport). While at Sport Canada, Dr. Dallaire was responsible for the management of the Sport Science Support Program, which provided funding to more than forty national sport governing bodies, to support their sport science initiatives. He was also on the review panel for the Sport Science Research Program and served as the liaison between the government of Canada and the Sports Medicine Council of Canada and its four professional member organizations.

Dr. Dallaire relocated to the U.S. in 1992 to develop a comprehensive performance enhancement program—Human Performance International—where he served as president for eight years.

In 1998 he moved to the Charlotte, NC, area where he ultimately formed Performance Prime and currently serves as its president.

Over the past forty years, Dr. Dallaire has enjoyed the opportunity to work directly with nearly seven hundred high-performance motor racing drivers from forty-three countries, in addition to many hundreds of high-performance individuals from a multitude of sports and a variety of occupations, including law enforcement, the movie and entertainment world, and the business community.

Dr. Dallaire splits his time between delivering sports-team and corporate-group performance programs and giving individual one-on-one programs with high-performance competitors. He is a founding member of the International Council of Motorsport Sciences, a board member of the Stand 21 "Racing Goes Safer" Foundation, a member of the American College of Sports Medicine, and in 2007 was inducted into the Canadian Motorsports Hall of Fame—in recognition of his innovative, state-of-the-art training strategies and the impact he has had on the sport.